35th Edition

Mutual Fund

1995
FACT BOOK

▮◖ INVESTMENT COMPANY INSTITUTE

74108

3 9902 00049 2803

Thirty-fifth Edition
Copyright © 1995 by Investment Company Institute
ISBN 1-878731-14-9

Table of Contents

List of Figures

How to Use This Book

The 1995 Mutual Fund Fact Book is a basic guide to the trends and statistics that were observed and recorded during 1994. The Fact Book is divided into two main sections—text and data. A glossary appears at the end of the text section.

TEXT

The first part of the book covers the general history and development of the industry, key benefits and features of mutual funds, and how they are sold, plus 1994 trends in mutual funds. Charts, graphs, and tables illustrating sales, assets, redemptions, exchanges, and other trends help you compare 1994 to prior years. To locate specific charts, graphs, and tables in this part of the book, refer to the index on page 143.

DATA

The blue pages, starting on page 98, identify the data section, which has its own table of contents to help you find specific information quickly. Each table in this section is clearly labeled by classification, for example, Industry Totals, Long-term Funds, Short-term Funds, etc. If you cannot find the data you need in the table of contents for the data section, refer to the index on page 143.

As you use the *Fact Book,* keep in mind that the industry usually divides its statistics into two broad categories: long-term funds (stock and bond & income funds) and short-term funds (taxable and tax-exempt money market funds). To obtain the total industry picture, refer to the notes that may appear at the bottom of the tables in both the text and data sections (the blue pages). For example, in the Long-term Funds section, a note at the bottom of the page will refer you to comparable short-term data or total industry data.

The Industry Totals data section (pages 101 to 102) includes information on shareholder assets, accounts, and numbers of funds. Industry totals are broken down from the short- and long-term categories into four separate ones: equity funds, bond and income funds, taxable money market funds, and tax-exempt money market funds; this breakdown should give you a more detailed picture of industry activity.

The Industry Totals section does not provide total sales figures that combine long-term and short-term fund sales. Because of the special nature of short-term funds and the huge, continuous inflows and outflows of money they experience, it would be misleading to add their sales figures to those of long-term funds. Tracking periodic changes in total assets is usually the preferred method for following trends of short-term funds.

Other data sections cover long-term funds, short-term funds, exchanges, retirement plans, and institutional investors in more detail. Some data are broken down by investment objective. The Institute identifies 21 major categories of investment objectives, which are defined on pages 17 and 18.

The Economic And Financial Environment In 1994

A strong U.S. economy translated into good and bad news for households and financial institutions in 1994. In most respects, the economy's performance was outstanding, experiencing robust growth, declining unemployment, and relatively low and stable inflation.

These favorable developments, however, did not lead to ideal financial market conditions. In general, the rising interest rate environment produced relatively flat stock prices and an especially volatile bond market. As a result, long-term, fixed-income investors generally suffered the most, as bond prices declined more in 1994 than in any year dating to 1969.

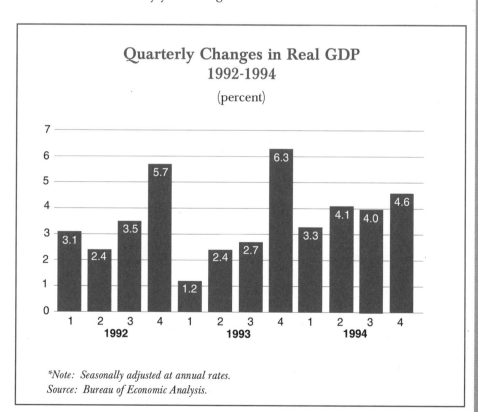

Quarterly Changes in Real GDP
1992-1994

(percent)

*Note: Seasonally adjusted at annual rates.
Source: Bureau of Economic Analysis.

STRONG ECONOMIC PERFORMANCE

The U.S. economy experienced a broad-based expansion in 1994. Gross domestic product (GDP), the output of goods and services produced in the United States, grew at a real (inflation-adjusted) rate of 4 percent after rising 3.1 percent in 1993.

GDP growth, which experienced its largest annual increase since 1984, was relatively balanced throughout 1994, and the driving force was the growth of business fixed investment. Spending on capital equipment was particularly impressive, increasing 17.5 percent last year on the heels of an 18 percent rise in 1993.

Strong employment gains accompanied the increased economic activity. The unemployment rate declined from 6.4 to 5.4 percent, a level many economists considered within the range where inflationary pressures could have emerged. About 3.5 million new nonagricultural payroll jobs were created, an average of 290,000 per month.

Despite the favorable employment and other economic numbers, inflation was, by most measures, moderate during 1994. As measured by the consumer price index (CPI), inflation (2.7 percent) stayed under 3 percent for the third consecutive year, a situation not seen since the 1960s. The producer price index (PPI) increased 1.7 percent in 1994, while core CPI and PPI, which exclude food and energy, increased only 2.6 and 1.6 percent, respectively.

MONETARY POLICY AND INTEREST RATES

With the continuing strength of economic activity and the absence of any appreciable slack in labor markets, the Federal Reserve tightened U.S. monetary policy to ward off the threat of inflation. Although there were few signs of inflation

1994 Monetary Tightening by the Federal Reserve

	Federal Funds Rate	Discount Rate
February 4	From 3.00% to 3.25%	—
March 22	From 3.25% to 3.50%	—
April 8	From 3.50% to 3.75%	—
May 17	From 3.75% to 4.25%	From 3.00% to 3.50%
August 16	From 4.25% to 4.75%	From 3.50% to 4.00%
November 15	From 4.75% to 5.50%	From 4.00% to 4.75%

Source: Federal Reserve Board

in 1994, the Fed believed that the strong economy, if left unchecked, would fuel out-of-control economic growth.

The Fed boosted the federal funds rate, the overnight lending rate among banks, six times between February and mid-November, from 3 to 5.5 percent. The Fed also tacked on 1.75 percentage points to the discount rate, the rate it charges to member banks.

Short-term interest rates increased across the board during the year. The yield on the average 3-month CD rose from 3.3 to 6.3 percent, while that of the 3-month U.S. Treasury bill jumped from 3.1 to 5.6 percent. Long-term interest rates increased as well—but less than short-term rates—rising by an average of 1.5 percentage points. For example, the 30-year U.S. Treasury bond yield moved from 6.3 to 7.9 percent, while corporate bond rates were up from 6.9 to 8.5 percent. As a result, differences between short- and long-term interest rates narrowed during 1994, as shown in the chart.

THE INVESTMENT MARKETS

Fixed-income investors were hard hit by financial developments in 1994, especially the rising interest rate environment. The tightening Fed monetary policy,

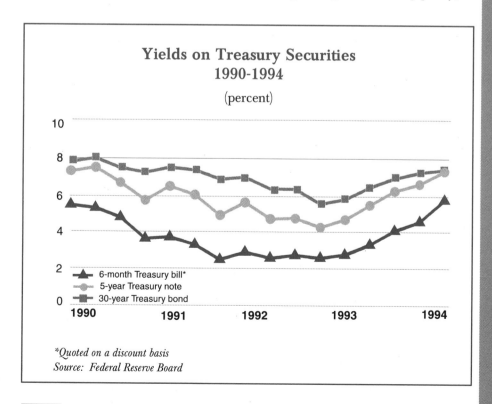

**Yields on Treasury Securities
1990-1994**

(percent)

- 6-month Treasury bill*
- 5-year Treasury note
- 30-year Treasury bond

*Quoted on a discount basis
Source: Federal Reserve Board

expectations of still higher interest rates, and strong economic growth caused prices of fixed-income securities to fall across the board.

The total return on bonds, as measured by the Salomon Brothers Broad Bond Index, declined 2.9 percent, compared with a 9.9 percent gain in 1993. Long-term corporate bonds, as measured by Salomon Brothers High-Grade Bond Index, dropped by 5.7 percent, compared with a 13.2 percent gain in 1993.

Meanwhile, the stock market was lackluster. For example, the broad-based Standard & Poor's 500 Composite Index registered only a 1.3 percent gain, compared with its 10.1 percent return in 1993.

Performances of long-term mutual funds were generally disappointing in 1994. The average fixed-income fund total return, as calculated by Lipper Analytical Services, was negative 3.3 percent, compared with a 9.7 percent gain in 1993. Equity funds, also according to Lipper figures, posted a modest 2.3 percent gain, down from an 18.8 percent figure for 1993.

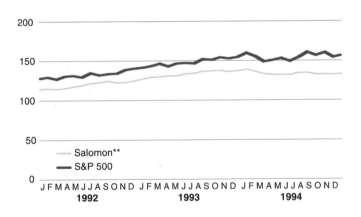

Total Return Indexes of Stocks and Bonds*
1992-1994

Salomon**
S&P 500

JFMAMJJASOND JFMAMJJASOND JFMAMJJASOND
1992 **1993** **1994**

Note: December 1990 = 100
* Total Return includes appreciation and investment income and equals the percent change in the index.
** Includes Treasury/government-sponsored bonds, corporate bonds, and mortgage-backed securities.
Source: Salomon Brothers and Standard & Poor's Inc.

MUTUAL FUND ASSET GROWTH

Assets in long-term mutual funds increased only 2.7 percent in 1994, compared with a 37.3 percent gain during the previous year. Bond and income fund assets declined from $761.1 billion to $684 billion (off 10.1 percent). In 1993, by comparison, bond and income fund assets rose 31.8 percent. Equity fund assets rose 15.7 percent, reaching a record-high of $866.4 billion.

New sales (total sales less reinvested dividends) of bond and income funds were $177 billion, the third-best annual figure on record. However, since redemptions were a record $187.8 billion, net new sales (new sales less redemptions) decreased $10.8 billion, compared with 1993's record $118.5 billion increase. Combined with net bond and income fund exchanges (exchanges in minus exchanges out) of negative $32.7 billion, net new cash flow (new sales minus redemptions plus net exchanges) was down $43.4 billion, the first negative figure for bond and income funds since 1988.

Equity fund new sales reached a record $257.6 billion level, and, with redemptions at $141.9 billion, equity funds delivered net new sales of $115.7 billion. Since net exchanges for equity funds increased $3.6 billion, net new cash inflow was $119.3 billion, second only to 1993's record high of $129.6 billion.

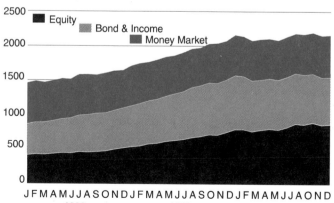

Total Net Assets of All Mutual Funds
1992-1994

(billions of dollars)

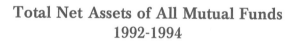

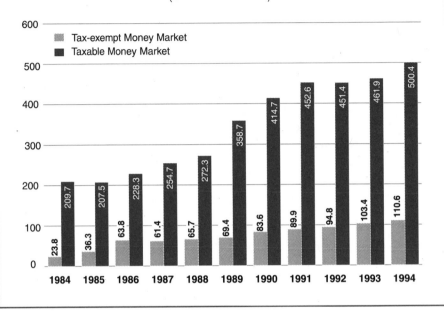

Total Net Assets of Taxable and Tax-exempt Money Market Funds
1984-1994
(billions of dollars)

Legend:
- Tax-exempt Money Market
- Taxable Money Market

Year	Tax-exempt Money Market	Taxable Money Market
1984	23.8	209.7
1985	36.3	207.5
1986	63.8	228.3
1987	61.4	254.7
1988	65.7	272.3
1989	69.4	358.7
1990	83.6	414.7
1991	89.9	452.6
1992	94.8	451.4
1993	103.4	461.9
1994	110.6	500.4

Money market funds, riding the tide of rising short-term interest rates, had their best asset year since 1991. Money market fund assets rose to a record $611 billion, an 8.1 percent increase, compared with a 3.5 percent gain in 1993. Taxable money market fund assets increased by $38.5 billion (8.3 percent), while short-term tax-exempt fund assets rose $7.2 billion (7 percent).

How Mutual Funds Contribute To The U.S. Economy

The mutual fund industry acts as an important bridge between American investors and securities issuers. Consequently, it helps millions of mutual fund shareholders reach their investment goals, while at the same time assisting U.S. economic growth through participation in the various capital markets.

The mutual fund industry's presence as a major force on the U.S. economic landscape is undeniable. Over the past dozen years, it has grown into the nation's second largest financial intermediary, with $2.16 trillion in assets.

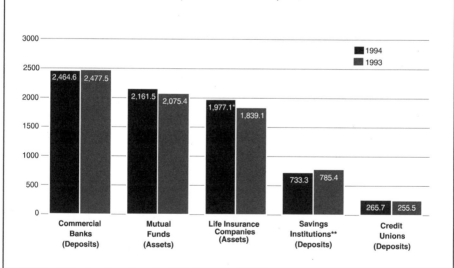

Total Deposits and Assets of Selected Financial Intermediaries, 1993-1994

(billions of dollars)

Legend: ■ 1994 ■ 1993

	1994	1993
Commercial Banks (Deposits)	2,464.6	2,477.5
Mutual Funds (Assets)	2,161.5	2,075.4
Life Insurance Companies (Assets)	1,977.1*	1,839.1
Savings Institutions** (Deposits)	733.3	785.4
Credit Unions (Deposits)	265.7	255.5

* Estimated by American Council of Life Insurance (ACLI)
** Includes savings and loan associations, mutual savings banks, and federal savings banks.
Source: Federal Reserve Board, ACLI, and the ICI.

MUTUAL FUNDS INFLUENCE
INDIVIDUAL CAPITAL MARKETS

The mutual fund industry promotes U.S. economic growth through its increasing participation in the short- and long-term financial markets.

The Money Market. Mutual funds breathe new life into the money market, the investment arena where institutions, such as banks, corporations, and governments, finance short-term borrowing. Increasing demand for money market investments from mutual fund investors allows institutional borrowers to lower the cost of debt.

Mutual Fund Assets as a % of the Open-market Paper Market

43.1

1994

Source: Federal Reserve

Small- and medium-sized businesses have been particular beneficiaries of lower short-term credit costs. For example, today's vigorous market for commercial paper (i.e., short-term loans to corporations) relates directly to the rapid growth of money market funds over the past 20 years. Over the past ten years, both short- and long-term mutual funds maintained high asset levels in open-market paper (i.e., commercial paper and banker's acceptances). By yearend 1994, mutual funds owned $268.8 billion worth of open-market paper, which represents 43.1 percent of that market.

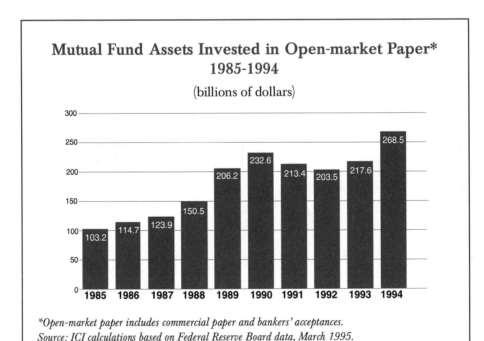

Mutual Fund Assets Invested in Open-market Paper*
1985-1994

(billions of dollars)

Year	Value
1985	103.2
1986	114.7
1987	123.9
1988	150.5
1989	206.2
1990	232.6
1991	213.4
1992	203.5
1993	217.6
1994	268.5

Open-market paper includes commercial paper and bankers' acceptances.
Source: ICI calculations based on Federal Reserve Board data, March 1995.

Mutual Fund Assets as a % of Corporate & Foreign Bond Markets

7.2

1994

Source: Federal Reserve

The Bond Market. Many of the same players in the money market finance debt in the long-term bond market. As with the money market, an expanding mutual fund presence in the domestic and foreign fixed-income markets has broadened the availability and lowered the cost of long-term institutional borrowing.

In 1994, for example, mutual funds held $173.5 billion in bonds issued by foreign and domestic corporations. Over the past ten years, mutual fund assets in the foreign and domestic debt issues have risen dramatically, from 2.2 percent of the market in 1984 to 7.2 percent by yearend 1994.

Mutual funds also helped expand the market for securitized mortgage loans, increasing the availability of residential mortgage financing for homeowners and lowering the cost of financing home purchases for millions of American families. Mortgage-backed securities include those issued by the Government National Mortgage Association (Ginnie Mae), the Federal National Mortgage Association (Fannie Mae), and the Federal Home Loan Mortgage Corporation (Freddie Mac).

Since bonds issued by states and local governments are typically exempt from federal as well as individual state income taxes, the municipal bond market con-

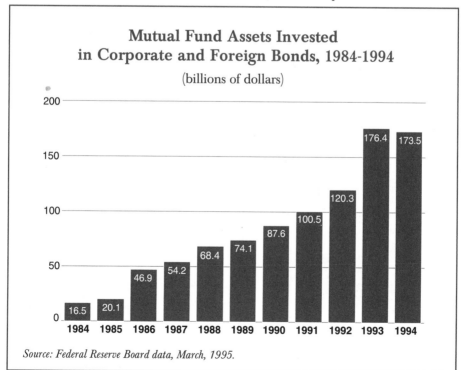

Mutual Fund Assets Invested in Corporate and Foreign Bonds, 1984-1994

(billions of dollars)

Year	Value
1984	16.5
1985	20.1
1986	46.9
1987	54.2
1988	68.4
1989	74.1
1990	87.6
1991	100.5
1992	120.3
1993	176.4
1994	173.5

Source: Federal Reserve Board data, March, 1995.

tinues to attract heavy demand from mutual fund investors. As a result, municipal bond mutual funds assist the financing of important public projects, such as roads, bridges, libraries, and schools.

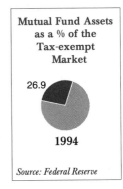
And as investors have continued to search for ways to reduce taxes over the past decade, the mutual fund industry's assets in the municipal market have increased almost four-fold, rising from $69.8 billion in 1985 to $323.2 billion in 1994. Furthermore, combined assets in short- and long-term municipal bond funds rank the mutual fund industry as the second largest holder of municipal securities behind individual investors.

The Stock Market. Mutual funds also contribute to economic growth through their participation in equity markets. Without mutual fund participation in the stock market, many initial public offerings might not otherwise proceed. Through their investments, mutual funds help finance job creation and provide capital to build American infrastructure.

Mutual fund assets in corporate equities reached an all-time high in 1994, $737.7 billion, more than 10 percent higher than the previous record in 1993. Furthermore, stock mutual fund assets are more than five times higher than the $113.7 billion gathered ten years ago.

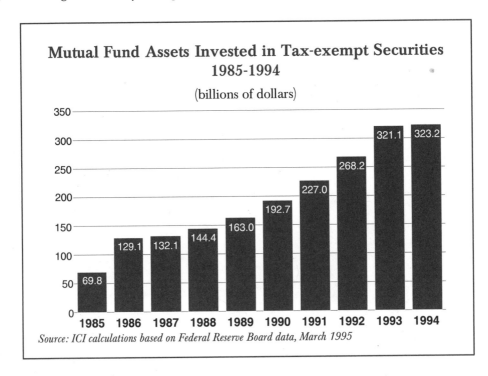

Mutual Fund Assets Invested in Tax-exempt Securities 1985-1994

(billions of dollars)

Source: ICI calculations based on Federal Reserve Board data, March 1995

As with the money and bond markets, increased mutual fund investing has stimulated many stock market issues, making it simpler and cheaper for new companies to finance their growth. The greater upside potential of these companies makes them quite attractive among investors, who held $110.4 and $228.8 billion worth of assets in aggressive growth funds and growth funds, respectively, at yearend 1994.

Mutual Fund Assets as a % of the Corporate Equity Market

12.2

1994

Source: Federal Reserve

A GROWING INVESTMENT CHOICE IN AMERICAN HOUSEHOLDS

Since 1940, when Congress enacted the Investment Company Act, the mutual fund industry has grown from 68 funds to more than 5,000 funds, and increased assets from $448 million to about $2.2 trillion.

Furthermore, mutual funds have developed into important investment vehicles for U.S. investors, serving more than 38 million individual shareholders and representing 31 percent of U.S. households. Mutual funds' share of household discretionary assets (i.e., relatively liquid assets that can be readily converted into cash) has increased in recent years as well. According to Federal Reserve statis-

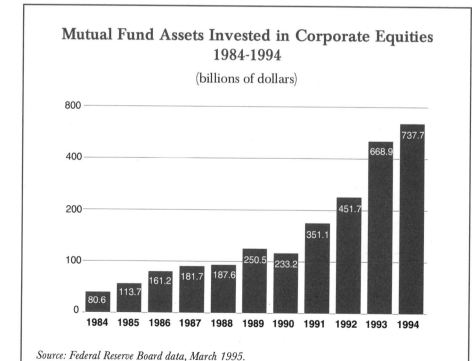

Mutual Fund Assets Invested in Corporate Equities 1984-1994

(billions of dollars)

Year	Value
1984	80.6
1985	113.7
1986	161.2
1987	181.7
1988	187.6
1989	250.5
1990	233.2
1991	351.1
1992	451.7
1993	668.9
1994	737.7

Source: Federal Reserve Board data, March 1995.

tics, household discretionary assets invested in mutual funds totaled $1.3 trillion in 1994, or 15 percent of total household discretionary assets; these figures are up from $826.4 billion, or 12 percent of household discretionary assets, in 1990.

What Is a Mutual Fund?

THE BASICS

A mutual fund is a company that invests on behalf of individuals and institutions with similar financial goals.

Pooling is the key to mutual fund investing. By combining the financial resources of thousands of shareholders–each with a different amount invested–all of a mutual fund's investors realize the same benefits: professional money management, diversified ownership in securities markets, and a variety of services not otherwise available to most individuals. The total number of fund shares outstanding changes from day to day as a mutual fund issues new shares when more money is invested, and as the fund redeems, or buys back, shares from investors who need to sell all or part of their investment.

Professional money managers invest the pool of assets in a variety of stocks, bonds, or other securities selected from a broad range of industries, government agencies, and authorities. In effect, each mutual fund investor then owns a percentage of the portfolio created by the fund's money managers.

Fund managers decide when to buy, sell, or hold securities based on extensive research. They consider the financial health of individual security issuers as well as general economic and market trends, and rely on data from a variety of economic and statistical resources.

If the securities in the investment portfolio appreciate in value, or pay dividends or interest, all the fund's investors reap their proportionate share of the rewards. For example, investors who put $1,000 in the fund get the same rate of return, or yield per share, as those investing $100,000.

Money managers select securities that best meet their fund's investment objective, as explained in the fund's prospectus. Investment objectives are usually described in terms of one or more main goals. These may include stability–protecting an investor's principal (the initial amount invested) from loss; growth–increasing the value of the principal; and income–generating a regular stream of income through dividends.

The investment objective set forth by a mutual fund is critical to both the fund manager and the investor. The manager uses it as a guide when choosing investments for the fund's portfolio. Investors use it to determine which funds are suitable for their needs. Mutual fund investment objectives vary widely, ranging from maximizing return (with correspondingly higher risk) to providing the highest level of income consistent with the preservation of an investor's principal. The Investment Company Institute classifies mutual funds according to 21 major investment objectives. (For a definition of each, see pages 17-18.)

To achieve their objectives, fund managers may invest in dozens of securities, seeking diversification among companies, industries, governments, and other organizations and institutions to reduce an investor's principal risk.

Some funds, known as sector or specialty funds, may choose to diversify their investments more narrowly: within a specialized segment of the securities markets. For example, funds may invest in a particular industry, such as health care services, technology, energy, or utilities. Other funds may focus on particular segments of the economy, such as small businesses or real estate, or securities from certain geographic regions. Still other funds may invest only in companies that meet certain social criteria. Some funds may even invest in other mutual funds.

A mutual fund whose investment selections have a narrow focus tends to be more volatile than the markets as a whole. Although these specialty mutual funds are less diversified than many other mutual funds, investing in them will provide greater diversification *within* that sector than investing in just one or two individual securities.

The Investment Company Institute compiles lists of 18 different specialty fund categories. Descriptions of those categories, as well as an index of funds within each category, are included in ICI's annual *Directory of Mutual Funds* (see the order form on page 157 at the back of this book).

EARNING MONEY THROUGH FUNDS

Mutual funds make money for their shareholders in three ways. First, if the overall value of securities held by a fund increases, the value of the fund's portfolio—and therefore the value of each mutual fund share—increases as well. Of course, the investor won't realize the increase until shares are sold. Second, mutual funds may pay dividends to shareholders. For example, if a fund's investment objective is current income, it will invest in stocks or bonds expected to produce current dividends or interest. The fund then passes through these earnings to its shareholders in the form of dividends. These distributions are typically made monthly, quarterly, or annually, depending on the type of fund.

Types of Mutual Funds

Aggressive Growth Funds seek maximum capital appreciation (a rise in share price); current income is not a significant factor. Some funds in this category may invest in out-of-the-mainstream stocks, such as those of fledgling or struggling companies, or those in new or temporarily out-of-favor industries. Some of these funds may also use specialized investment techniques such as option writing or short-term trading. For these reasons, these funds usually entail greater risk than the overall mutual fund universe.

Balanced Funds generally try to balance three different objectives: moderate long-term growth of capital, moderate income, and moderate stability in an investor's principal. To reach these goals, balanced funds invest in a mixture of stocks, bonds, and money market instruments.

Corporate Bond Funds seek a high level of income by purchasing primarily bonds of U.S.-based corporations; they may also invest in other fixed-income securities such as U.S. Treasury bonds.

Flexible Portfolio Funds may invest in any one investment class (stocks, bonds, or money market instruments) or any combination thereof, depending on the conditions in each market. Because they do not limit a fund manager's exposure to any one market, these funds provide the greatest flexibility in anticipating or responding to economic changes.

Ginnie Mae or GNMA Funds seek a high level of income by investing primarily in mortgage securities backed by the Government National Mortgage Association (GNMA). To qualify for this category, the majority of a fund's portfolio must always be invested in mortgage-backed securities.

Global Bond Funds seek a high level of income by investing in the debt securities of companies and countries worldwide, including issuers in the U.S. The funds' money managers deal with varied currencies, languages, time zones, laws and regulations, and business customs and practices. Because of these factors, although global funds provide added diversification, they are also subject to more risk than domestic (U.S.) bond funds.

Global Equity Funds seek capital appreciation (a rise in share price) by investing in securities traded worldwide, including issuers in the U.S. These funds operate just like other global and international funds (see above), providing added diversification but also added risk.

Growth and Income Funds invest mainly in the common stock of companies that offer potentially increasing value as well as consistent dividend payments. Such funds attempt to provide investors with long-term capital growth and a steady stream of income.

Growth Funds invest in the common stock of companies that offer potentially rising share prices. These funds primarily aim to provide capital appreciation (a rise in share price) rather than steady income.

High-yield Bond Funds maintain at least two thirds of their portfolios in noninvestment-grade corporate bonds (those rated Baa or lower by Moody's rating service and BBB or lower by Standard and Poor's rating service). In return for potentially greater income, high-yield funds present investors with greater credit risk than do higher-rated bond funds.

Income-Bond Funds seek a high level of income by investing in a mixture of corporate and government bonds.

Income-Equity Funds seek a high level of income by investing primarily in stocks of companies with a consistent history of dividend payments.

Income-Mixed Funds seek a high level of current income by investing in income-producing securities, including both equities and debt instruments.

International Funds seek capital appreciation (a rise in share price) by investing in equity securities of companies located outside the U.S. Two thirds of fund assets must be so invested at all times to qualify for this category.

National Municipal Bond Funds–Long-term invest primarily in bonds issued by states and municipalities to finance schools, highways, hospitals, airports, bridges, water and sewer works, and other public projects. In most cases, income earned on these securities is not taxed by the federal government, and may or may not be taxed by state and local governments. For some taxpayers, a portion of income may be subject to the federal alternative minimum tax.

Precious Metals/Gold Funds seek capital appreciation (a rise in share price) by investing at least two thirds of fund assets in securities associated with gold, silver, and other precious metals.

State Municipal Bond Funds–Long-term work just like national municipal bond funds (see previous page) except that their portfolios primarily contain the issues of one state. For residents of that state, the income from these securities is typically free from both federal and state taxes. For some taxpayers, a portion of income may be subject to the federal alternative minimum tax.

Taxable Money Market Mutual Funds seek the highest income consistent with preserving investment principal. These funds seek to maintain a stable $1.00 share price by investing in short-term money market securities (a portfolio's average maturity must be 90 days or less) of the highest credit quality. Examples of money market securities include U.S. Treasury bills, commercial paper (short-term IOUs) of

corporations, and large-denomination certificates of deposit (CDs) of banks. Because of their short-term, high-quality characteristics, money market funds are considered the lowest risk mutual funds available.

Tax-exempt Money Market Funds–National seek the highest level of federally tax-free income consistent with preserving investment principal. These funds invest in short-term municipal securities issued by states and municipalities to finance local projects. For some taxpayers, a portion of income may be subject to the federal alternative minimum tax.

Tax-exempt Money Market Funds–State work just like other tax-exempt money market funds (see above) except that their portfolios invest primarily in issues from one state. A resident in that state typically receives income exempt from federal and state taxes. For some taxpayers, a portion of income may be subject to the federal alternative minimum tax.

U.S. Government Income Funds seek income by investing in a variety of U.S. Government securities, including Treasury bonds, federally guaranteed mortgage-backed securities, and other government-backed issues.

Third, if a fund manager sells a security that has increased in value, shareholders receive capital gain distributions. Capital gain distributions are generally paid out annually.

Shareholders may choose to reinvest dividends and capital gains in the purchase of additional fund shares or they can ask the fund company to send them a check for the amount of earnings.

SHARE PRICING

When investors pool their money in a mutual fund, their dollars buy shares in that fund. To determine the price of these shares, at the close of every business day the fund company adds up the value, after expenses, of all securities held in the fund's portfolio. It then divides that total by the number of shares outstanding. Thus, the price is determined by the actual market value of the holdings in the portfolio, rather than by the volume of shares bought or sold by shareholders. Unlike a traditional corporation, mutual funds may issue an unlimited number of shares. In addition, shareholders may redeem part or all of their holdings at any time.

Each day, the fund must figure the value of its portfolio and how many shares are outstanding. Those simple calculations determine a fund's Net Asset Value (NAV). Because it represents the value of a single share in the fund, the NAV is important to know when a fund shareholder either redeems or purchases shares. Daily NAVs appear in the financial pages of most major metropolitan newspapers.

Individual fund shareholders may determine the value of their holdings by simply multiplying the number of shares they own by the NAV. Although the NAV may not seem to change much over time, dividend and capital gain reinvestments can contribute toward buying many more shares than originally purchased. So, even if the NAV does not change a great deal, owning more shares represents an increase in the value of the shareholder's investment.

SHARE TAXATION

Under the Internal Revenue Code, mutual funds that meet certain requirements serve as conduits through which the income and gain earned from underlying portfolio securities passes through to shareholders without any tax due from the fund. Any income or capital gain taxes, by law, are also passed on to the fund's shareholders, who generally treat long-term capital gains earned by the fund as capital gain income, and the remainder of the fund's income (including the taxable dividends and interest that the fund earns) as ordinary income. Income from certain securities is exempt from federal, state, or local taxes.

For tax purposes, shareholders receive a yearend statement from the fund showing clearly what part of the money distributed to them represents ordinary income and what part represents long-term capital gains. The distinction between ordinary income and capital gains is important for two reasons. First, long-term capital gains are taxed at a maximum rate of 28 percent while ordinary income can be taxed at higher rates. Second, capital gains can be offset by capital losses.

Shareholders also receive regular statements from the fund that show the value of their investments, and periodic reports that detail the fund's progress, specific portfolio holdings, expenses, changes in management, and other relevant data.

HOW A FUND IS ORGANIZED

A mutual fund is owned by its shareholders. A board of directors elected by the shareholders is responsible for the fund's investment policies and objectives. The board appoints officers to manage daily operations or delegates that function to a management company.

The management company, often the organization that created the fund, may offer any number of mutual funds, each with a different investment objective. Some funds may have separate classes, or fee structures, to meet different investor needs. The management company may also offer other financial products and services (see Chapter 6 for a fuller description). The management company usually serves as the fund's investment adviser, or money manager.

An investment adviser is usually paid to manage a fund's portfolio through a fee based on a percentage of the total value of assets managed. Investment management fees average about one half of 1 percent annually. Since other operating expenses are usually near that amount, a fund's entire cost of operations typically averages about 1 percent per year. Since fees are taken out of a fund's earnings, they are a factor in a fund's total return. (See pages 45-47 for a more detailed discussion of fees.)

Besides the investment adviser, the fund also typically contracts with a custodian, a transfer agent, and a principal underwriter. The custodian is usually a bank whose functions include safeguarding the fund's assets, making payments for the fund's securities, and receiving payments when securities are sold. The transfer agent performs recordkeeping services for shareholders: it issues new shares, cancels redeemed shares, and distributes dividends and capital gains to shareholders. The principal underwriter arranges for the distribution and marketing of new fund shares to the investing public. An underwriter may act as a wholesaler, selling fund shares to securities dealers, or as a retailer, selling directly to the public.

HOW FUNDS ARE DISTRIBUTED TO THE PUBLIC

Fund shares reach the public in a variety of ways. However, funds are generally distributed either directly to the public or through a sales force, such as a brokerage firm, a bank, an insurance company, or a financial planning firm.

Regardless of the method chosen, investors must understand that mutual funds, unlike bank deposits, are not insured or guaranteed by the Federal Deposit Insurance Corporation or any other government agency. Neither are mutual funds guaranteed by the bank or other financial institution through which the fund investment is made. Mutual funds involve investment risk, including the possible loss of principal; of course, investment risk always carries the potential for greater reward as well.

Funds that market shares directly to the public often use advertising and direct mail. Their shares are usually distributed with a small sales commission or none at all. In some cases, the fund's directors may authorize the use of a small percentage of fund assets to support distribution efforts. Known as a 12b-1 fee, it is named for the Securities and Exchange Commission (SEC) rule that permits it.

Fund shares marketed through a sales force may be offered by registered representatives such as brokers, financial planners, and insurance agents, or, in some cases, through sales employees of a fund organization. All of these representatives may be compensated through a direct sales commission included in the fund's share price, through a 12b-1 distribution fee paid by the fund, or in both ways.

All mutual fund activities are highly regulated. Mutual funds must register with the SEC pursuant to the Investment Company Act of 1940, and are regulated under this statute and other federal securities laws. Funds are also regulated under state securities laws (called blue sky laws) in all states where securities are sold (see Chapter 9 for more information on mutual fund regulation).

Historical Background

America's mutual fund industry has enjoyed enormous success since the first fund was introduced in Boston in 1924.

That fund, and the great many that followed, grew out of a concept dating to 19th-century England. Money invested in English and Scottish investment companies (or trusts, as they are known there) had helped finance the post-Civil War economy in America. Shareholders of these British investment companies financed U.S. farm mortgages as well as railroads and other industries.

In the early 1920s, as the U.S. industrial revolution reached full swing, Americans were presented with increasing investment opportunities. Several financial firms, mostly bankers, brokers, and investment counselors located in New York, Boston, and Philadelphia, tried to meet expanding investor needs. Soon thereafter, mutual funds joined these firms in the competition for investor preference.

Shortly after the first funds were organized, however, the 1929 stock market crash ravaged the U.S. financial markets. Despite setbacks, many efficiently managed investment companies maintained their pattern of growth and service, and the industry grew dramatically over the years.

In 1936, under congressional mandate, the Securities and Exchange Commission (SEC) undertook a special study of investment companies that culminated in the Investment Company Act of 1940. Soon afterward, industry professionals who had worked closely with the SEC to draft the 1940 Act decided to form a permanent committee that cooperated with the federal regulatory agency. Together, they formulated rules and regulations that would implement the spirit of the 1940 Act. The committee, a pioneering group called the National Committee of Investment Companies (NCIC), also kept informed of trends in state and federal mutual fund legislation.

As the scope of their activities increased, the NCIC leadership decided in October 1941 to change the organization's name to the National Association of Investment Companies (NAIC). Besides disseminating information to the public, the NAIC began acting as a liaison with the SEC, monitoring mutual fund legislation and helping maintain high industry standards. In 1961, the NAIC changed its name to the Investment Company Institute (ICI); in 1970, the ICI moved its headquarters from New York to Washington, DC.

The ICI marked its 50th anniversary in October 1990, and during that span the mutual fund industry has experienced staggering growth. From $448 million in assets under management and 296,000 shareholder accounts in 1940, the industry quickly reached marks of $1 billion in assets in 1945 and one million accounts in 1951. By the early 1970s, the industry comprised nearly 400 funds and more than $50 billion in assets. At the end of 1994, the industry had grown to more than 5,300 funds with more than $2.1 trillion in assets. As a result, investment companies are now the nation's second largest financial intermediary, surpassed in size only by commercial banks.

Initially, mutual funds had carved out a niche among stock market investors, but in the early 1970s a new concept–money market fund investing–signaled a dramatic industry change. This novel approach let investors with limited financial resources reap the high short-term interest rates of the money market, a profitable arena previously reserved only for major institutions and wealthy individuals.

The money market mutual fund significantly altered our nation's financial services landscape. Most importantly, it attracted new investors to the mutual fund concept; some individuals had never put their money in anything more than a passbook savings account. Also, money market funds sparked a surge of creativity in the industry. Tax-exempt money market funds were introduced in 1979, a by-product of the Tax Reform Act of 1976. U.S. Government bond and Ginnie Mae funds followed quickly after in the early 1980s, and specialty or sector funds mushroomed throughout that decade. Index, adjustable rate mortgage (ARM), and international funds are just a few of the popular products that have surfaced even more recently.

Into the 1990s, the mutual fund industry has continued to grow and prosper despite periods of securities market volatility. Furthermore, through dedication to a very simple proposition–that innovative investment products could offer investors diversification and professional management at a reasonable cost–the investment company industry has played a significant role in opening the securities markets to more than 38 million individual investors.

CHAPTER 4

Growth and Development

Shifts in the distribution of mutual fund assets that began in the early 1980s have continued into the 1990s. In 1982 and prior years, assets were heavily concentrated in money market mutual funds, a result of rising interest rates, low stock prices, and recession. Money market funds, introduced in 1972, became highly popular by providing investors with market rate yields in the late 1970s as interest rates surged to double digits.

By 1984, the percentage of assets in money market funds began to decline. In 1984, taxable money market funds represented 56.6 percent of all mutual fund assets, significantly less than two years earlier (69.6 percent in 1982). Equity funds in 1984 represented 22.4 percent of all fund assets, bond and income funds were 14.6 percent, and tax-exempt money market funds were 6.4 percent.

By yearend 1994, almost three quarters of total net mutual fund assets were invested in long-term funds. Equity funds led the way, with 40.1 percent of industry assets. Bond and income fund assets dropped from 36.7 to 31.6 percent of industry assets during 1994 (most likely a reflection on the volatile conditions in the bond market for the year).

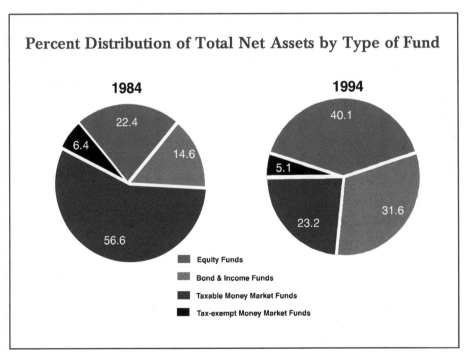

Percent Distribution of Total Net Assets by Type of Fund

1984

22.4
6.4
14.6
56.6

1994

40.1
5.1
31.6
23.2

- Equity Funds
- Bond & Income Funds
- Taxable Money Market Funds
- Tax-exempt Money Market Funds

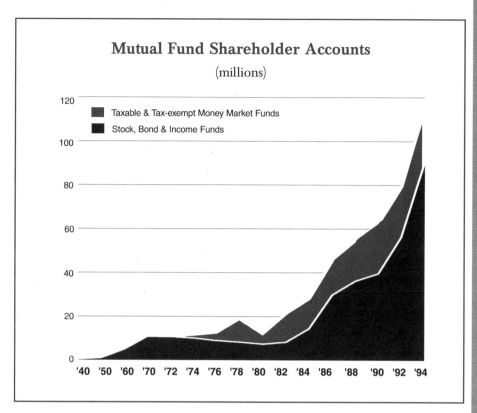

Mutual Fund Shareholder Accounts
(millions)

Legend:
- Taxable & Tax-exempt Money Market Funds
- Stock, Bond & Income Funds

X-axis: '40 '50 '60 '70 '72 '74 '76 '78 '80 '82 '84 '86 '88 '90 '92 '94

Y-axis: 0, 20, 40, 60, 80, 100, 120

Taxable money market funds, meanwhile, represented 23.2 percent of mutual fund assets in 1994, a substantial shift compared to a decade ago. Tax-exempt money market funds represented 5.1 percent of the industry's assets compared with 6.4 percent in 1984.

Investor confidence in the equity and bond markets wavered only slightly in 1994. In 1994, net sales of equity and bond and income funds followed 1993's all-time high of $280.2 billion by dropping to $144.2 billion. Still, the 1990s have brought continued prosperity to the industry, and 1994 net sales were the fourth highest figure ever.

Total industry assets also skyrocketed in the past ten years, growing from $370.7 billion at the end of 1984, passing the $1 trillion mark for the first time in 1990, and hovering at $2.16 trillion at the end of 1994. Taxable and tax-exempt money market fund assets reached the $500 billion level for the first time late in 1990, dipping back to $498 billion at yearend 1990. Nevertheless, taxable and tax-exempt money market fund assets grew to $611 billion by the end of 1994, up 23 percent from yearend 1990.

Taxable money market fund assets grew by $38.5 billion between yearend 1993 and 1994, to a total of $500.4 billion. Over the past ten years, taxable money

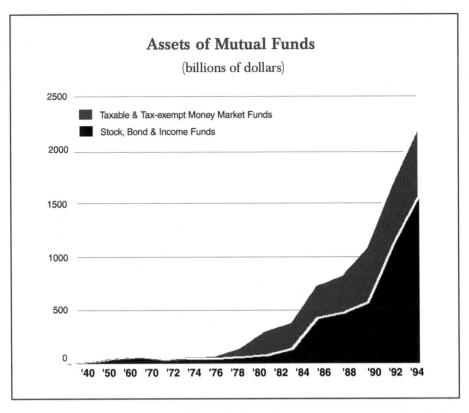

Assets of Mutual Funds
(billions of dollars)

Legend:
- Taxable & Tax-exempt Money Market Funds
- Stock, Bond & Income Funds

Y-axis: 0, 500, 1000, 1500, 2000, 2500

X-axis: '40 '50 '60 '70 '72 '74 '76 '78 '80 '82 '84 '86 '88 '90 '92 '94

market fund assets increased by $290.7 billion. Tax-exempt money market funds developed from $23.8 billion in assets at the end of 1984 to $110.6 billion as of yearend 1994.

Equity fund assets grew from $83.1 billion in 1984 to an all-time high of $866.4 billion at the end of 1994. In 1994, equity funds proved to be very popular among investors, growing $117.4 billion, or 16 percent, from the previous year despite a lackluster market. Bond and income fund assets dropped off from their record level at yearend 1993 ($761.1 billion), but still enjoyed a major expansion during the last ten years, growing from $54 billion in 1984 to $684 billion at the end of 1994. Bond and income fund assets dropped $77.1 billion, or 10 percent, between 1993 and 1994.

NUMBER OF FUNDS INCREASES DRAMATICALLY

As the economic environment changed during the past two decades, the mutual fund industry responded by introducing new products and services to meet a number of investment objectives and investor goals, and to provide choice and selection in the fund industry. In the 1950s and 1960s, steep increases in sales and assets of equity funds reflected the industry's historic concentration in these

Sales, Redemptions, and Assets

(billions of dollars)

Equity and Bond & Income Funds

Year	Sales	Redemptions	Net Sales	Assets
1979	$6.8	$8.0	$(1.2)	$49.0
1980	10.0	8.2	1.8	58.4
1981	9.7	7.5	2.2	55.2
1982	15.7	7.6	8.1	76.9
1983	40.3	14.7	25.6	113.6
1984	45.9	20.0	25.9	137.1
1985	114.3	33.8	80.5	251.7
1986	215.8	67.0	148.8	424.1
1987	190.6	116.2	74.4	453.8
1988	95.3	92.5	2.8	472.3
1989	125.7	91.7	34.0	553.9
1990	149.5	98.2	51.3	568.5
1991	236.6	116.3	120.3	853.0
1992	364.4	165.5	198.9	1,100.1
1993	511.6	231.4	280.2	1,510.1
1994	474.0	329.7	144.2	1,550.5

Taxable Money Market Funds

Year	Sales	Redemptions	Net Sales	Assets
1979	$111.9	$78.4	$33.5	$45.2
1980	232.2	204.1	28.1	74.5
1981	451.9	346.7	105.2	181.9
1982	581.8	559.6	22.2	206.6
1983	463.0	508.7	(45.7)	162.6
1984	572.0	531.1	40.9	209.7
1985	730.1	732.3	(2.2)	207.5
1986	792.3	776.3	16.0	228.3
1987	869.1	865.7	3.4	254.7
1988	903.4	899.4	4.0	272.3
1989	1,134.6	1,055.1	79.5	358.7
1990	1,218.9	1,183.1	35.8	414.7
1991	1,569.9	1,536.5	33.4	452.6
1992	2,099.8	2,101.3	(1.5)	451.4
1993	2,335.6	2,336.9	(1.3)	461.9
1994	2,233.9	2,228.9	5.0	500.4

Tax-exempt Money Market Funds

Year	Sales	Redemptions	Net Sales	Assets
1980	$5.3	$3.8	$1.5	$1.9
1981	10.5	8.3	2.2	4.3
1982	29.4	22.2	7.2	13.2
1983	44.5	42.4	2.1	16.8
1984	62.3	55.9	6.4	23.8
1985	109.4	98.8	10.6	36.3
1986	197.5	172.3	25.2	63.8
1987	191.9	196.9	(5.0)	61.4
1988	178.3	175.0	3.3	65.7
1989	184.8	180.5	4.3	69.4
1990	196.8	189.6	7.2	83.6
1991	230.9	226.6	4.3	89.9
1992	286.5	281.6	4.9	94.8
1993	341.9	336.5	5.4	103.4
1994	369.4	370.1	(0.7)	110.6

Net Exchanges by Investment Objective–1994

(millions of dollars)

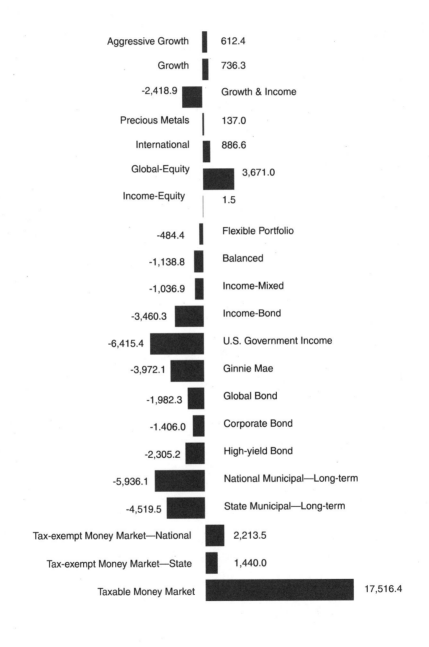

Aggressive Growth	612.4
Growth	736.3
-2,418.9	Growth & Income
Precious Metals	137.0
International	886.6
Global-Equity	3,671.0
Income-Equity	1.5
-484.4	Flexible Portfolio
-1,138.8	Balanced
-1,036.9	Income-Mixed
-3,460.3	Income-Bond
-6,415.4	U.S. Government Income
-3,972.1	Ginnie Mae
-1,982.3	Global Bond
-1.406.0	Corporate Bond
-2,305.2	High-yield Bond
-5,936.1	National Municipal—Long-term
-4,519.5	State Municipal—Long-term
Tax-exempt Money Market—National	2,213.5
Tax-exempt Money Market—State	1,440.0
Taxable Money Market	17,516.4

funds. This growth occurred in a period when stock prices rose steadily with only slight interruptions.

However, from 1968 to 1974, a weak stock market, rising interest rates, inflation, and other economic and financial uncertainties heightened concerns about risks associated with equities, dimming investor willingness to wait for long-term, higher returns from equity funds. Consequently, investors stepped away from stocks and equity mutual funds and moved toward the relative safety of short-term liquid assets.

Taxable money market mutual funds were developed in 1972, and their tax-exempt counterparts were introduced in 1979. Tax-exempt money market mutual funds enabled more individual and institutional investors to enter the short-term municipal bond market. In addition to tax-exempt money market funds, new versions of standard stock and bond funds, such as international funds, precious metals funds, and, more recently, Ginnie Mae and government income funds were created. Since 1980, there has been a net increase of almost 4,800 funds. In 1994 alone, nearly 800 new funds appeared, and the total number reached 5,357.

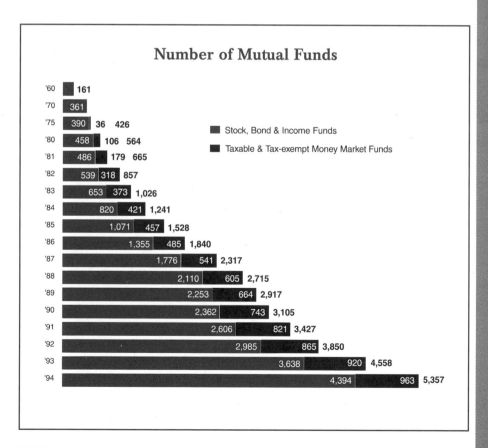

Number of Mutual Funds

'60 161
'70 361
'75 390 36 426
'80 458 106 564
'81 486 179 665
'82 539 318 857
'83 653 373 1,026
'84 820 421 1,241
'85 1,071 457 1,528
'86 1,355 485 1,840
'87 1,776 541 2,317
'88 2,110 605 2,715
'89 2,253 664 2,917
'90 2,362 743 3,105
'91 2,606 821 3,427
'92 2,985 865 3,850
'93 3,638 920 4,558
'94 4,394 963 5,357

■ Stock, Bond & Income Funds
■ Taxable & Tax-exempt Money Market Funds

The enormous growth and diversity of funds has led to the development of new fund categories or investment objectives. Currently, the Investment Company Institute classifies industry funds in 21 different investment objectives. Prior to 1984, the Institute classified funds into only 10 categories. By broadening its product line and encouraging the use of the exchange feature within a family of funds, the mutual fund industry has transformed itself into a diversified financial business capable of providing a variety of benefits to individual and institutional investors under all kinds of economic conditions.

SALES OF MUTUAL FUNDS CONTINUE TO BE HIGH

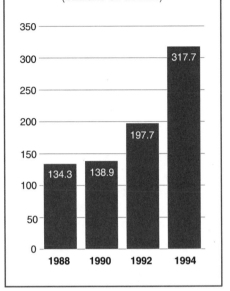

**Sales Exchanges
All Types of Mutual
Funds**

(billions of dollars)

Mutual fund sales continue to demonstrate investor confidence. Despite the tumultuous financial market environment, sales of equity and bond and income funds were substantial in 1994. Following three consecutive record years, sales in 1994 were $474 billion, down 7 percent from the $511.6 billion record for the previous year. (See the *Sales, Redemptions, and Assets* table on page 27).

In the late 1980s, exchanges became more popular than ever. Investors continued to show an awareness of this feature, which allows mutual fund shareholders to exchange shares from one fund to another within a family of funds. Shareholders use the exchange feature to shift investments depending on individual goals, and to take advantage of financial market conditions. For instance, in 1994, interest rates started to rise, and bond fund values declined. At the same time, money market funds performed relatively well, a result of the rise in short-term interest rates. Activity was high in the stock, bond, and money market sectors, with asset growth in money market funds especially robust.

In 1994, exchanges into all types of mutual funds totaled $317.7 billion, the highest level ever, and a 28 percent increase over the previous record of $249 billion in sales exchanges recorded in 1993. In general, exchange activity over the decade has occurred between long-term equity and bond funds and short-term

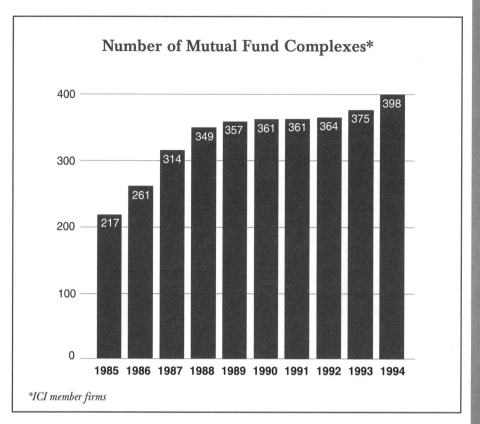

Number of Mutual Fund Complexes*

Year	Value
1985	217
1986	261
1987	314
1988	349
1989	357
1990	361
1991	361
1992	364
1993	375
1994	398

*ICI member firms

money market funds as investors adjust their assets to correspond to their changing needs and to reflect their view of current market conditions.

In a relatively short time, mutual funds have become the nation's second largest type of financial institution, with assets exceeded only by those of commercial banks (see Chapter 2 for more information about how mutual funds contribute to the financial markets).

Services to Meet Investor Needs

The ability to take an innovative approach to complex financial markets is one of the hallmarks of the mutual fund industry. Furthermore, by keeping attuned to investor needs, the mutual fund industry has adapted and expanded its product line and services to suit just about any investor's goals.

The number of funds and investment objectives has grown dramatically over the past two decades. In 1975, 426 mutual funds fit neatly into seven main categories recognized by the Investment Company Institute (ICI); by the end of 1985, 1,528 funds comprised 16 ICI categories. In many cases, individual fund companies chose to specialize investment objectives even further, creating investment portfolios, for example, based on industry sectors, geographic limitations, or business philosophies.

As a result, the number of mutual funds has more than tripled between 1985 and yearend 1994, to 5,357, and the ICI now recognizes 21 wide-ranging investment objectives.

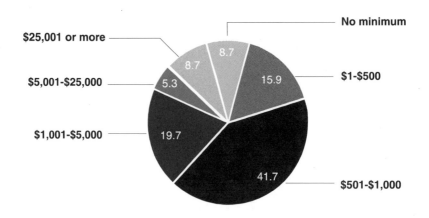

Minimum Investment Requirements

(percent distribution of funds by minimum investment requirement*)

Many mutual funds offer lower investment minimums for Individual Retirement Accounts and automatic investment plans.

ACCOUNT OPTIONS

Almost every fund company establishes minimum initial account sizes as well as minimums for subsequent investments. Some offer very low or no initial minimums; others have minimums of $5,000 or more. Large institutional funds may have minimums of $1 million or more. The great majority of fund accounts for individuals, however, can be opened with amounts of $1,000 or less. (See the graph on page 32.)

Fund organizations try to make investing as easy as possible. Many offer payroll deduction plans for those interested in investing regularly, and some fund companies, upon an investor's authorization, will deduct a specified amount from a personal bank account.

Mutual funds also offer programs through which shareholders can automatically reinvest dividend and capital gain distributions in the purchase of new fund shares to expand their holdings. Automatic withdrawals work in much the same way. A fund company sends checks regularly, from account earnings or principal, to the shareholder or anyone else designated by the shareholder.

Whether or not a shareholder participates in a regular plan, withdrawing mutual fund assets is easy. By law, the fund must be ready to redeem shares on any business day. A shareholder needs only to authorize a transaction, and a fund representative will send a check or electronically wire the proceeds to a personal bank account. Many funds also offer the convenience of checkwriting, although most fund companies limit draft amounts to $250 or more.

Many management companies that offer a family of funds (often with different objectives) typically allow convenient exchange privileges. Thus, investors may quickly adjust their fund allocation within a fund family based on changing personal investment objectives or shifting market conditions. Usually, fund companies permit exchanges several times a year at no charge, or for a low fee per exchange.

With shareholder authorization, most funds allow exchanges by telephone. An investor can execute a telephone exchange, usually for a minimum exchange amount, in a matter of minutes.

ACCOUNT RECORDKEEPING AND INFORMATION

Whenever a mutual fund investor redeems or invests shares—through exchanges, checkwriting, wiring, or other means—a statement is sent to confirm the transac-

Number of Mutual Funds
Classified by Investment Objective

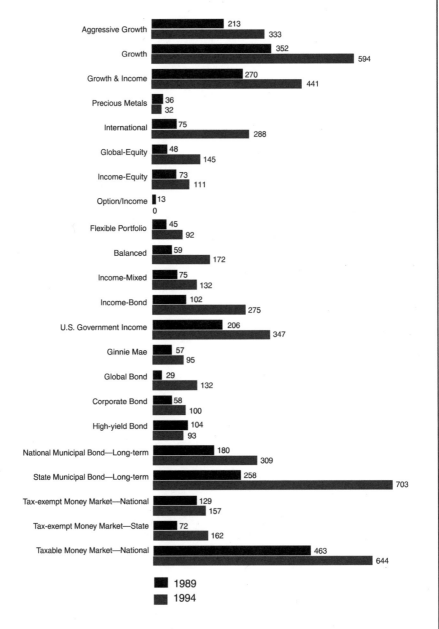

Category	1989	1994
Aggressive Growth	213	333
Growth	352	594
Growth & Income	270	441
Precious Metals	36	32
International	75	288
Global-Equity	48	145
Income-Equity	73	111
Option/Income	13	0
Flexible Portfolio	45	92
Balanced	59	172
Income-Mixed	75	132
Income-Bond	102	275
U.S. Government Income	206	347
Ginnie Mae	57	95
Global Bond	29	132
Corporate Bond	58	100
High-yield Bond	104	93
National Municipal Bond—Long-term	180	309
State Municipal Bond—Long-term	258	703
Tax-exempt Money Market—National	129	157
Tax-exempt Money Market—State	72	162
Taxable Money Market—National	463	644

■ 1989
■ 1994

Note: In 1989, there were 13 funds in the Option/Income category. As of January 1992, funds in this category were reclassified as Income-Equity.

tion. Mutual funds also send account summaries, or statements, usually on a monthly, quarterly, or annual basis.

Besides account updates, funds often send a shareholder newsletter, a valuable resource for keeping abreast of investments and fund services. Newsletters, typically sent quarterly, contain items that educate or inform through discussions of economic trends, taxes, fund performance, and personal financial planning.

Finally, funds send periodic financial reports to shareholders that are also filed with the Securities and Exchange Commission. These investment updates must be sent at least every six months during a fund's fiscal year (some funds do not report on a calendar year). These reports are valuable snapshots, detailing a fund's complete investment portfolio; discussing investment strategy and performance for the reporting period; and including independently audited financial statements and related information.

Many funds also offer services that enhance retirement and other long-term financial planning. For example, salary reduction pension plans or Individual Retirement Accounts (IRAs) are just two of the ways to incorporate mutual funds into an overall long-term strategy (see Chapter 14 for more information on the topic of mutual funds and retirement).

The mutual fund industry continually harnesses cutting-edge technology to provide efficient and professional service. For example, many fund companies are now exploring the benefits of personal computers as a means to share information with current and prospective shareholders. Another technological enhancement, the voice-response telephone system, lets shareholders retrieve fund and account information, or even perform simple transactions, 24 hours a day.

The mutual fund industry constantly aims to meet the needs of its customers. And judging by the healthy competition that exists within the industry, that objective seems likely to remain a priority, leading to continually better products and services for all investors.

Professional Management

Considered one of the most attractive mutual fund features, professional management is perhaps more crucial than ever in today's investment environment. For many individuals who have neither the time nor the resources to invest directly in the securities markets, mutual funds can provide welcome relief from the daunting task of portfolio planning.

Even those preferring to invest directly may sometimes feel squeezed by the institutionalization of the securities market. Institutions play an overarching role in the markets through volume trading, which can dramatically affect securities prices. Changes in corporate governance, boards of directors, takeover activity, and other dynamics can also cause rapid fluctuations in securities prices. In such a complex environment, the average investor may find it difficult to determine which individual securities and industries benefit or suffer.

To invest more effectively, therefore, increasing numbers of Americans rely on the professional money management that mutual funds provide. In this way, no matter how modest their holdings, individuals can join institutions as integral players in the financial markets.

WHAT DO THE FUND MANAGERS DO?

Fund managers are charged with the complex task of making educated investment decisions based on a predetermined investment objective, prominently disclosed in the fund's prospectus.

Portfolio managers invest the pool of investor assets in dozens of securities, attempting to diffuse an investment portfolio's volatility while meeting its

Taxable Money Market Fund Asset Composition Yearend 1994

(billions of dollars)

U.S. Treasury Bills	$44.3
Other Treasury Securities	23.3
Other U.S. Securities	78.9
Repurchase Agreements	69.7
Commercial Bank CDs	6.7
Other Domestic CDs	15.8
Eurodollar CDs	16.0
Commercial Paper	189.5
Bankers' Acceptances	2.4
Cash Reserves	(2.6)
Other	56.4
Total Net Assets	**$500.4**
Average Maturity (days)	34
Number of Funds	644

objectives. A fund's management, often a team of individuals, gathers extensive economic data and financial research to ensure that informed decisions are made when building or adjusting a fund's portfolio.

The roles of individuals on a fund management team may vary. Certain investment analysts, for example, might research basic economic trends, such as inflation or interest rates, to determine how securities issuers will be affected. On a stock fund management team, one member may be an expert on utilities, while another colleague is well versed on the computer industry or overseas markets.

All fund managers must keep up with an endless stream of data that securities issuers release to the public or file with government agencies. Fund managers study balance sheets and other financial statements provided by individual issuers, and investigate product lines and marketing philosophies, often talking to a cross-section of a company's employees.

DIVERSIFYING ASSETS

Typically, portfolio managers will invest the pool of shareholder assets in anywhere from 50 to 200 different securities to diversify the fund's holdings. As such, they might be charged with the task of diversifying millions, even billions, of investor dollars.

While providing an attractive return (within the parameters of the fund's investment objective) is important, diversifying assets serves to reduce the impact of the volatility of any individual security in the fund's portfolio. Diversification is a proven method of reducing investment risk.

Diversification can be approached in many ways:

■ **By numbers of securities**–Federal and state regulations require certain levels of diversification. The Investment Company Act of 1940 sets minimum diversification standards that a mutual fund must meet to qualify as a diversified investment company; the Internal Revenue Code mandates similar measures that funds must meet to qualify as a

Portfolio Composition of Equity and Bond & Income Funds Yearend 1994
(billions of dollars)

Common Stock	$812.2
Preferred Stock	16.5
Warrants and Rights	0.8
Options	(0.4)
Municipal Bonds (long-term)	210.3
Municipal Bonds (short-term)	5.9
Other Taxable Debt	157.2
U.S. Gov't Sec. (long-term)	222.2
U.S. Gov't Sec. (short-term)	19.1
Liquid Assets	96.4
Other	10.3
Total Net Assets	**$1,550.5**

regulated investment company. States also may impose diversification requirements that must be met before funds can offer shares within their boundaries. The Securities and Exchange Commission prohibits taxable money market mutual funds from investing more than 5 percent of assets in the securities of any one issuer.

■ **Among different types of securities**–Balanced funds (see "Types of Funds" on page 17) employ this strategy, for example; such funds may invest in common and preferred stocks, bonds, and money market instruments in the interests of taking diversification to a very broad level.

■ **Across industries or markets**–Stock funds, in particular, may diversify assets among security issues spanning various industries. Such an approach may give a fund performance characteristics that closely resemble the stock market in general. Bond funds might include issues of various markets. For example, one bond fund could invest in securities issued in mortgage-backed, U.S. government, and the corporate bond markets; tax-free bond funds might include securities issued by a wide range of state and local governments.

■ **Within maturity ranges**–Bond and money market funds typically diversify assets in securities of differing maturities. Depending upon market conditions, a fund's average maturity, short- or long-term, may strongly influence performance.

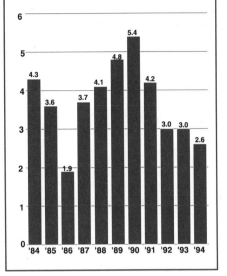

**Consumer Price Index
1984-1994**

(percent)

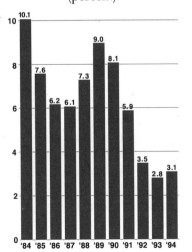

**Taxable Money Market
Funds Average Annual
Yield**

(percent)

Some funds diversify less than others. Specialty or sector funds, for example, may focus on a specific industry, market segment, or geographic region. A narrowly defined bond fund may invest in fixed- and adjustable-rate mortgage securities (ARM funds); a specialized stock fund might target technology firms, the health care industry, emerging markets, or companies whose products are environmentally safe. Specialty funds are typically more volatile than funds that invest more broadly, but still diversify within their specific areas of interest.

A VAST ARRAY OF CHOICES

The huge volume of mutual fund transactions over the past ten years has been a major source of liquidity in the securities markets; it has also helped attract new security issuers to the various markets.

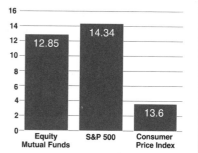

Mutual Fund Investment Performance–Ten Years Through 12/31/94

(percent)

Note: Mutual fund performance reflects a monthly weighted average for all equity funds. Mutual fund and S&P 500 data are prepared by Lipper Analytic Services. These indices are not adjusted for sales charges.

Mutual fund managers must now choose from thousands of U.S. equity issues with an estimated value of more than $5.5 trillion, plus thousands more issues from foreign exchanges. At the close of 1994, mutual funds owned $812.2 billion worth of stocks from around the world.

The table on page 42 details how equity fund managers allocated assets to various industry sectors during 1994. As might be expected, a manager's preference for certain industries may change from year to year.

Mutual funds also purchase substantial quantities of bonds, helping finance the debt of corporate America as well as that of state and local governments. Mutual funds held $157.2 billion in corporate and other taxable fixed-income issues and $210.3 billion in long-term municipal debt at the end of 1994. The mutual fund industry has also become an important buyer of government-backed mortgage securities, Treasury bonds, and other government and agency issues. Mutual funds currently hold about $241.2 billion worth of these securities in their portfolios.

SOURCES OF EARNINGS

A mutual fund's management, according to the predetermined investment objective(s) found in the fund prospectus, delivers earnings to investors chiefly through three sources: price appreciation, dividend income, and capital gain distributions.

Price appreciation. If the total value of the securities in a fund's portfolio increases, so does the price of an investor's shares. If the total value of the securities in a portfolio decreases, so does the value of a shareholder's principal investment. Stocks are typically chosen for their price appreciation potential. Bonds, although they are chiefly looked on as a source of dividend income, may be chosen by a portfolio manager for their price appreciation potential as well.

Dividend distributions. Mutual funds pay out income earned on the securities in their investment portfolios. Fixed-income investments, such as bond and money market funds, typically pay dividends more often than stock funds. Stock fund managers may also choose stocks for their income-paying (or dividend) potential.

Dividends and Reinvestment–All Types of Mutual Funds
(billions of dollars)

Year	Investment Income Dividends	Reinvested Dividends	Percent Reinvested
1977	$1.9	$1.3	65.8%
1978	2.5	1.8	71.3
1979	5.2	3.7	72.2
1980	10.4	8.5	81.3
1981	21.7	19.7	91.7
1982	25.8	22.9	88.8
1983	18.8	15.7	83.5
1984	23.7	18.4	77.6
1985	28.9	20.4	70.6
1986	35.8	25.5	71.2
1987	47.4	30.9	65.2
1988	52.6	33.2	63.1
1989	62.7	43.6	69.5
1990	63.0	47.5	75.4
1991	64.0	47.1	73.6
1992	79.5	45.1	56.7
1993	92.5	49.9	53.9
1994	85.2	56.1	65.8

Capital Gain and Dividend Distributions to Shareholders All Types of Mutual Funds

(billions of dollars)

Year	Net Realized Capital Gains	Net Investment Income		
		Equity and Bond & Income Funds	Money Market Funds	Tax-exempt Money Market Funds
1977	$0.6	$1.8	$0.1	-
1978	0.7	2.1	0.4	-
1979	0.9	2.5	2.7	-
1980	1.8	2.7	7.7	$0.1
1981	2.7	3.1	18.5	0.1
1982	2.4	3.8	21.7	0.3
1983	4.4	5.0	13.2	0.6
1984	6.0	7.2	15.4	1.0
1985	5.0	12.9	14.4	1.6
1986	17.5	22.3	11.1	2.4
1987	23.0	31.8	12.8	2.8
988	6.3	32.0	17.3	3.5
1989	14.8	34.1	24.7	3.9
1990	8.1	32.9	26.3	3.8
1991	14.1	35.3	25.2	3.5
1992	22.3	59.2	17.2	3.1
1993	36.1	73.3	15.9	3.3
1994	30.0	61.5	20.5	3.2

Capital gain distributions. If a fund profits from selling securities during a year, the fund pays shareholders the resulting proceeds in distributions typically made once or twice a year.

For those mutual funds that provide investors with the potential for income, shareholders must decide whether to reinvest dividend and capital gain distributions in the purchase of additional shares of the fund, or take the gains as cash. When a mutual fund shareholder reinvests income or capital gain distributions, they, in effect, earn income on their income, and the value of their investment compounds.

Diversification of Mutual Funds
Common Stock Holdings by Sector

	1993		1994	
	Dollars (millions)	**Percent**	**Dollars (millions)**	**Percent**
Utilities	$39,302	13.2%	$38,236.5	10.1%
Energy	30,383	10.2	31,138.5	8.3
Financials	53,470	17.9	63,115.7	16.7
Industrial Cyclical	42,022	14.1	57,247.3	15.2
Consumer Durables	20,704	6.9	25,229.6	6.7
Consumer Staples	11,037	3.7	18,425.6	4.9
Services	30,096	10.1	32,105.3	8.5
Retail	18,292	6.1	14,743.5	3.9
Health	15,773	5.3	26,167.2	6.9
Technology	37,249	12.5	70,882.9	18.8
Total	**$298,328**	**100.0%**	**$377,292.1**	**100.0%**

Note: Composite sector investments drawn from the portfolios of the 60 largest investment companies reported by Morningstar, Inc. as of yearend 1993 and 1994. Total assets of the companies represent approximately 40 and 43 percent of total net assets of all equity companies in 1993 and 1994, respectively.

Source: Morningstar, Inc.; calculations by ICI.

The majority of mutual fund shareholders choose to reinvest their dividends and capital gains. In 1994, investors reinvested $56.1 billion, or 65.8 percent, of the $85.2 billion of investment income that they received from their mutual funds.

Equity and bond & income funds generated $61.5 billion of investment income in 1994, compared with $73.3 billion in 1993. Relative to other investments, long-term mutual funds have generally provided investors with higher returns, which many investors have enhanced through reinvested income.

Money market funds distributed $20.5 billion to shareholders in 1994, compared with $15.9 billion in 1993. Tax-exempt money market funds paid out $3.2 billion in 1994, compared with $3.3 billion in 1993.

How Mutual Fund Shares Are Acquired by Investors

Mutual funds are generally bought in one of two ways: directly from a fund company, i.e., *direct marketed*, or indirectly through a sales agent, i.e., *sales-force marketed*.

Direct marketed funds are sold through the mail, by telephone, or at office locations; sales-force marketed funds may be sold through securities firms, financial planners, life insurance companies, banks, or specific membership groups. Funds may also be offered as selections in employee benefit plans.

Nearly every securities firm distributing mutual fund shares, either retail or wholesale, is a member of the National Association of Securities Dealers, Inc. (NASD). This self-regulatory body of the securities industry polices the sales practices of its member firms, including how mutual fund shares are distributed.

Generally, a mutual fund underwriter decides which channels to use in reaching investors:

Broker/Dealers–The majority of mutual fund underwriters distribute fund shares through these agents, which are securities firms with a commissioned sales force.

Besides traditional broker/dealer firms, banks and independent financial planners are increasingly important distribution agents for mutual funds. Financial planners suggest mutual funds to their clients as fundamental building blocks in a master financial plan that might also include life insurance and individual securities. In recent years, banks have also begun to offer mutual fund products in addition to traditional savings accounts.

No matter where the fund is purchased, fund shares, unlike bank deposits, are not insured nor guaranteed by the Federal Deposit Insurance Corporation or any other government agency. Nor are they guaranteed by the bank or other financial institutions through which the investment is made. Like any other investment, mutual funds involve investment risk, including the possible loss of principal. Of course, investment risk always includes the potential for greater reward.

Sales of Sales Force & Direct Marketing Funds by Investment Objective–1994

(percent)

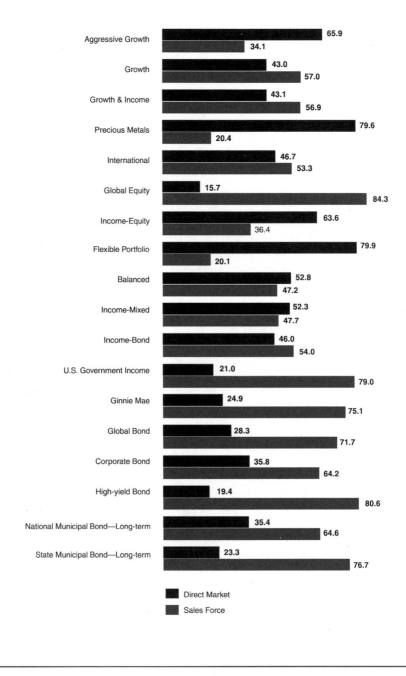

	Direct Market	Sales Force
Aggressive Growth	65.9	34.1
Growth	43.0	57.0
Growth & Income	43.1	56.9
Precious Metals	79.6	20.4
International	46.7	53.3
Global Equity	15.7	84.3
Income-Equity	63.6	36.4
Flexible Portfolio	79.9	20.1
Balanced	52.8	47.2
Income-Mixed	52.3	47.7
Income-Bond	46.0	54.0
U.S. Government Income	21.0	79.0
Ginnie Mae	24.9	75.1
Global Bond	28.3	71.7
Corporate Bond	35.8	64.2
High-yield Bond	19.4	80.6
National Municipal Bond—Long-term	35.4	64.6
State Municipal Bond—Long-term	23.3	76.7

Within the broker/dealer distribution system, underwriters, in effect, act as wholesalers. Underwriters do not sell shares to the public directly. Instead, they establish sales agreements with securities firms that, in turn, sell the fund's shares to individual investors through a firm's branch-office network. To assist local firms and branches, a mutual fund underwriter usually divides the country into regions and assigns its own staff members to represent the underwriter in each area.

Captive (or Dedicated) Sales Force–In some cases, an underwriter employs its own sales force, which primarily sells mutual fund shares along with other securities issued by the underwriter and its affiliates. Sometimes, a captive sales force is the sales arm of an insurance company that might own a mutual fund management company.

Direct-Marketed–Through this channel, investors purchase mutual fund shares directly from the fund. However, most direct-marketed funds also have an underwriter–a distribution arm of the fund organization through which all share transactions pass.

Direct marketers typically offer fund shares to the public with a low sales charge or none at all. Direct marketers do not usually offer specific investment advice; therefore, potential investors are required to do their own research and determine whether specific funds meet their needs. Investors contact the fund organization directly to obtain a prospectus or buy shares.

FEE INFORMATION

Like any other company, a mutual fund must pay for the normal costs of doing business (for example, expenses related to fund management, as well as to legal, accounting and shareholder services). These annual operating expenses are not paid directly by the investor, but are deducted from fund assets before earnings are distributed to shareholders. In general, the higher a fund's operating expenses, the lower the amount of earnings available for distribution to shareholders.

In addition, a commission or sales charge, also known as a "load," may be attached to mutual fund investments, usually when the shares are either purchased (at the "front end") or sold (at the "back end"). Fund shares sold through full-service distribution channels, such as brokers or financial planners, typically include a sales charge or fee of some sort in exchange for providing additional investment advice or services.

A sales charge may range up to 8.5 percent, although most fund families charge less than the maximum allowable front-end load. Usually the basic charge varies depending on the size of the purchase; some funds may also charge a fee on reinvested dividends.

CHANGING FEE STRUCTURES

In recent years, the mutual fund industry has developed an even greater variety of fee structures to respond to varying investor preferences.

In addition to, or in place of, a front-end load, some funds assign a small percentage of fund assets to offset distribution expenses. This charge is known as a 12b-1 fee (named after the Securities and Exchange Commission rule that permits it). Some funds sold through brokers or other sales professionals may include a 12b-1 fee structure to compensate the seller of fund shares, rather than through a front-end load (commission). Other funds may use the fee to pay for such distribution expenses as advertising.

Under NASD rules, 12b-1 fees cannot exceed 0.75 percent of a fund's average net assets per year. (An additional 0.25 percent service fee may be paid to brokers or other sales professionals in return for providing ongoing information and assistance to shareholders.) Furthermore, the NASD imposes a rolling cap on total sales charges, to be calculated at 6.25 percent of gross new sales for funds that pay an annual service fee, and 7.25 percent plus interest for funds that do not pay an annual service fee.

Disclosure of Fees and Charges

Information on all fees and charges is included in a table in the fund's prospectus. In reviewing the table, remember that, although they offset the return on a fund investment, fees should not be the sole consideration when selecting a mutual fund. For example, a fund with higher fees may make more money, even after expenses, than a fund with lower fees whose investments don't earn as much. Increased fees may reflect the costs of providing an expanded range of investor advice and services.

Often an annual 12b-1 fee is combined with a declining charge when shares are redeemed, a type of back-end load. For example, a contingent deferred sales charge (CDSC) is imposed if shares are redeemed during the first few years of ownership. The CDSC may be expressed as a percentage of either the original purchase price or the redemption proceeds. Most CDSCs decline over time, and if you remain in the fund long enough (typically anywhere from one to six years), the fee will not be charged. Any load–whether back-end or front-end–is a type of transaction fee.

Multiple-class fund shares constitute another form of fund ownership, and, in effect, an alternative sales charge arrangement among sales-force marketed funds. Multiple classes of shares represent ownership in the same portfolio of securities, but permit shareholders to choose the type of fee structure that meets their needs. For example, Class A shares might require payment of a front-end sales load, while Class B shares of the same fund might impose a contingent deferred sales charge and an annual 12b-1 fee instead of a front-end load. Class C shares might have annual 12b-1 and servicing fees, but no front-end or contingent deferred sales charge. Still other classes of shares may be offered to institutional investors, such as bank and trust departments, specifically designed to accommodate the needs of their individual beneficiaries.

SHARE REDEMPTION

Mutual funds are required to redeem outstanding shares at their current net asset value, which is usually calculated each afternoon after the close of business for U.S. security markets. (See page 19 for a discussion of net asset value.)

By law, mutual funds must stand ready to redeem any or all shares on any business day. Furthermore, a fund must send shareholders the proceeds within seven business days.

SALES BY METHOD OF DISTRIBUTION

Of all 1994 stock and bond and income fund sales, $243.2 billion or 51.3 percent are attributable to those funds distributed through a sales force. Stock and bond and income funds distributed directly to investors had sales of $191.5 billion, or 40.4 percent, of the total.

The two major distribution channels—sales force and direct marketing—recorded equity fund sales of $126.4 billion and $117.3 billion, respectively. Sales force distributors delivered $116.8 billion in bond and income fund sales, while direct marketers added $74.2 billion.

Regulation And Taxation

Within the framework of federal securities law, mutual fund organizations are perhaps the most strictly regulated business entities. A former chairman of the Securities and Exchange Commission (SEC) said, "No issuer of securities is subject to more detailed regulation than mutual funds."

The laws governing mutual funds require exhaustive disclosure to the SEC, state regulators, and fund shareholders, and entail continuous regulation of fund operations. Appropriately, however, these laws do not question the investment judgment of a fund's manager (provided the fund invests according to its stated objectives and any other restrictions set forth in its prospectus, as well as according to federal and state laws).

REGULATION OF FUNDS

Four major federal statutes regulate mutual funds.

The **Securities Act of 1933** requires a fund to file with the SEC a registration statement containing extensive information. This Act requires the fund to provide potential investors with a current prospectus, which contains detailed disclosure about the fund's management, investment policies, objectives, and other essential data. The 1933 Act also limits the type and content of advertisements that may be used by a mutual fund.

The purchase and sale of mutual fund shares, as with all securities, are subject to the antifraud provisions of the **Securities Exchange Act of 1934**. Mutual fund distributors are also regulated by the SEC and the National Association of Securities Dealers, Inc. (NASD) pursuant to the 1934 Act. The NASD is the self-regulatory organization for securities brokerage firms, including those that distribute mutual fund shares.

Another piece of federal legislation, the **Investment Advisers Act of 1940**, regulates the activities of investment advisers to mutual funds.

Finally, mutual funds must register with the SEC under the **Investment Company Act of 1940**, a highly detailed regulatory statute. The 1940 Act contains numerous provisions designed to prevent conflicts of interest, maintain the integrity of fund assets, and keep the fund and its shareholders from paying excessive fees and charges.

Most states also regulate mutual fund companies that sell shares within the state's boundaries. Both state and federal laws require appropriate disclosure to investors concerning the potential risks, returns, fees, and objectives associated with mutual funds. These laws are designed to ensure that mutual funds are operated and managed in the interests of their shareholders and that investors receive information enabling them to make appropriate investment decisions.

TAXATION OF SHAREHOLDERS

Unlike most corporations, a fund's income is generally taxed only once—when it is received by the shareholders, the actual owners of the securities. This pass-through tax treatment of income and capital gains is only available, however, to funds that qualify as regulated investment companies under Subchapter M of the Internal Revenue Code.

A fund must meet several Subchapter M requirements, including distributing 90 percent of its investment company taxable income each year and following various rules of asset diversification. A fund must also receive less than 30 percent of its gross income from the sale of securities held less than three months.

Once a fund meets Subchapter M requirements, earnings are then passed on to shareholders, and can be classified in several ways. A fund's short-term gains and other earnings are taxed to shareholders as ordinary income; its long-term capital gains are taxed to shareholders as long-term capital gains. Any tax-exempt income received by a fund is generally exempt from tax at the shareholder level as well.

Furthermore, fund income is generally taxed only when it is received by the shareholder. This one-level tax results from the deduction that funds receive for amounts distributed to shareholders. In addition, to avoid the imposition of an excise tax, a fund must generally distribute 98 percent of its income in the calendar year in which the income is earned.

CHAPTER 9

Recent Trends in Activity: Stock and Bond & Income Funds

The stock and bond & income fund sector of the mutual fund industry (long-term funds) continued to post strong sales in 1994. Although dropping off from the record pace in 1993 ($511.6 billion), sales of long-term funds totaled $474 billion, the second highest figure ever.

Continuing a trend evident throughout the 1990s, investors continued to pour discretionary assets into equity funds. Equity fund sales last year grew to an all-time high of $270.8 billion, up more than 18 percent from 1993's previous record of $228.8 billion.

Bond and income fund sales dropped off from the all-time high recorded in 1993. Sales volume was down 28 percent, to $203.2 billion, from the previous year's total of $282.8 billion.

Five of the seven equity fund categories listed by the Institute increased sales in 1994. In the growth and income fund category, still the largest equity fund classification, 1994 sales dropped 7.2 percent, from $71.2 billion to $66.2 billion. Sales of growth funds, the second largest stock fund category, were $56.8 billion, an 11 percent increase over the $51.2 billion figure for 1993. Aggressive growth fund

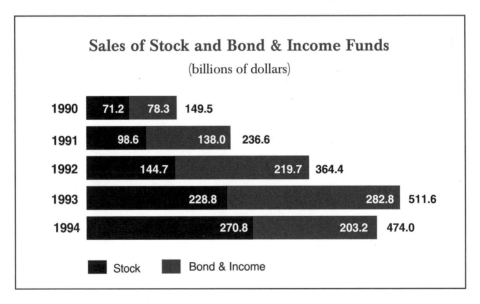

Sales of Stock and Bond & Income Funds

(billions of dollars)

1990	71.2	78.3	149.5
1991	98.6	138.0	236.6
1992	144.7	219.7	364.4
1993	228.8	282.8	511.6
1994	270.8	203.2	474.0

■ Stock   ■ Bond & Income

Share of Equity Funds
Sales and Redemptions Annually
(percent)

	Sales		Redemptions	
	1993	1994	1993	1994
Aggressive Growth	17.5%	19.6%	19.4%	19.7%
Growth	22.4	21.0	26.8	23.3
Growth & Income	31.1	24.4	33.7	27.1
Precious Metals	1.2	1.1	2.0	1.8
International	12.0	18.1	7.3	15.1
Global Equity	6.2	7.8	3.7	5.1
Income-Equity	9.6	8.0	7.1	7.9
Total	**100.0%**	**100.0%**	**100.0%**	**100.0%**

Share of Bond & Income Funds
Sales and Redemptions Annually
(percent)

	Sales		Redemptions	
	1993	1994	1993	1994
Flexible Portfolio	4.3%	8.0%	1.6%	3.8%
Balanced	7.0	9.3	3.5	5.6
Income-Mixed	10.7	15.2	10.8	10.4
Income-Bond	9.8	12.0	9.6	11.0
U.S. Government Income	16.0	11.4	22.0	18.8
Ginnie Mae	9.7	4.9	15.9	11.5
Global Bond	6.7	6.1	8.1	7.2
Corporate Bond	3.5	3.4	3.1	3.1
High-yield Bond	5.9	7.0	5.1	5.4
National Municipal Bond–Long-term	14.7	12.9	12.6	13.4
State Municipal Bond–Long-term	11.7	9.8	7.7	9.8
Total	**100.0%**	**100.0%**	**100.0%**	**100.0%**

sales followed a strong 1993 by rising 32.8 percent in 1994, from $40 billion to $53.1 billion.

International and global equity funds delivered the most dramatic rise, jumping approximately 77.9 and 48 percent, respectively. International funds remained the fourth largest equity sales category but closed in on third place, with approximately $49 billion total sales in 1994. Global equity funds also had a successful year, with sales jumping 48 percent from $14.2 billion to $21 billion in 1994.

Among the less popular equity categories for 1994, income-equity fund sales dropped 0.8 percent in 1994, finishing with sales of $21.7 billion. And rebounding from a drop in sales from 1993 to 1994, precious metals funds increased 6.3 percent to $2.9 billion in 1994.

Mutual Fund Assets
Classified by Investment Objective–Yearend
(billions of dollars)

Investment Objective	1993	1994	Percent Change
Aggressive Growth**	$123.7	$110.4	-10.8%
Growth	167.1	228.8	+36.9
Growth & Income	277.0	292.9	+5.7
Precious Metals	5.6	5.2	-7.1
International	71.0	101.8	+43.4
Global Equity	43.3	60.2	+39.0
Income-Equity	61.3	67.2	+9.6
Flexible Portfolio	35.0	44.3	+26.6
Balanced	58.0	59.2	+2.1
Income-Mixed	53.9	57.9	+7.4
Income-Bond	55.5	53.0	-4.5
U.S. Government Income	116.4	87.0	-25.3
Ginnie Mae	73.2	53.7	-26.6
Global Bond	38.2	31.4	-17.8
Corporate Bond	27.5	25.2	-8.4
High-yield Bond	48.7	45.1	-7.4
National Municipal Bond–Long-term	141.0	122.4	-13.2
State Municipal Bond–Long-term	113.6	104.8	-7.7
Total Long-term Funds*	**$1,510.0**	**$1,550.4**	**+2.7%**

*See next chapter for total short-term fund (taxable and tax-exempt money market funds) assets.
** As the result of annual reclassification of certain funds, approximately $40 billion in assets was shifted from the Aggressive Growth to Growth category during the year.

Reversing a trend from 1993, stock fund sales significantly outpaced those for bond and income funds. A volatile bond market environment contributed heavily to reduced inflows to bond and income funds in 1994; at $203.2 billion, bond and income fund sales were 25 percent lower than the sales of equity funds. In 1993, on the other hand, bond and income fund sales were outstanding, outpacing even the dramatic increases for equity funds.

Sales activity dropped in all but two of the 11 bond and income fund categories. Hardest hit were Ginnie Mae and U.S. Government income funds, which dropped 63.9 and 48.7 percent, respectively. U.S. Government income fund sales, which topped the bond and income category in 1993, were $23.2 billion in 1994, a figure that ranked only fourth best among bond and income funds.

Long-term municipal bond funds, both the state and national varieties, suffered as well. Sales of long-term state municipal bond funds, which dropped from

Mutual Fund Sales
Classified by Investment Objective–Yearend
(millions of dollars)

Investment Objective	1993	1994	Percent Change
Aggressive Growth	$39,974.9	$53,093.5	+32.8%
Growth	51,201.7	56,846.2	+11.0
Growth & Income	71,247.9	66,150.6	-7.2
Precious Metals	2,741.9	2,915.8	+6.3
International	27,538.4	48,994.4	+77.9
Global Equity	14,216.8	21,044.3	+48.0
Income-Equity	21,891.6	21,721.6	-0.8
Flexible Portfolio	12,142.5	16,210.4	+33.5
Balanced	19,896.7	18,785.6	-5.6
Income-Mixed	30,296.0	30,772.5	+1.6
Income-Bond	27,801.4	24,469.5	-12.0
U.S. Government Income	45,169.2	23,159.9	-48.7
Ginnie Mae	27,534.3	9,927.5	-63.9
Global Bond	19,031.2	12,441.4	-34.6
Corporate Bond	9,863.9	6,917.9	-29.9
High-yield Bond	16,659.3	14,291.8	-14.2
National Municipal Bond–Long-term	41,427.7	26,283.3	-36.6
State Municipal Bond–Long-term	32,943.1	19,949.5	-39.4
Total Long-term Funds*	**$511,578.5**	**$473,975.6**	**-7.4%**

*See next chapter for total short-term funds (taxable and tax-exempt money market funds) sales.

Sales and Redemptions
Equity Funds

(billions of dollars)

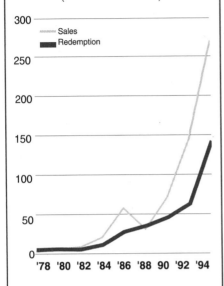

Sales and Redemptions
Bond & Income Funds

(billions of dollars)

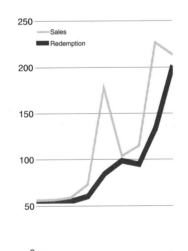

third to fifth largest bond and income fund sales category, declined 39 percent in 1994 after rising 37 percent the year before.

For the third consecutive year, flexible portfolio funds, which can invest in any combination of stocks, bonds, and money market funds, experienced outstanding sales growth. After two years of more than 100 percent growth, flexible portfolio fund sales rose 33.5 percent to $16.2 billion.

Sales of income-mixed funds totaled $30.8 billion, a 1.6 percent increase over the $30.3 billion in sales recorded in 1993. Income-bond funds dropped 12 percent, from $27.8 billion in 1993 to $24.5 billion in 1994. Balanced fund sales slipped to $18.8 billion, or 5.6 percent below the prior year.

Three of the smallest bond and income fund categories, the global, high-yield, and corporate varieties, saw sales drop by 34.6, 14.2, and 29.9 percent, respectively, during 1994. GNMA funds experienced the biggest sales declines, dropping 63.9 percent from 1993 to 1994.

The sales picture for long-term funds in 1994 indicates that mutual funds continue to be popular among investors, but the bond market caused some apprehension. Record redemptions reflect the changing condition in both the short- and long-term financial markets. Many investors moved into short-term funds in 1994, but, overall, the attractiveness and popularity of long-term funds seemed to hold steady.

Asset figures illustrate continued industry growth. Total long-term fund assets rose $40.3 billion in 1994, growing to $1.55 trillion from $1.51 trillion in 1993. Between 1991 and 1994, long-term fund assets have nearly doubled.

Yearend 1994 numbers show that total industry assets (long-term and short-term funds) hit an all-time high of $2.161 trillion, up $86 billion from the end of 1993. Since 1990, total industry assets have doubled, rising $1.095 trillion.

Shareholder account growth also testified to the industry's increased popularity. In 1994, there were 89.6 million equity and bond & income fund accounts, a 28 percent higher figure than at the close of 1993 and more than six times as many

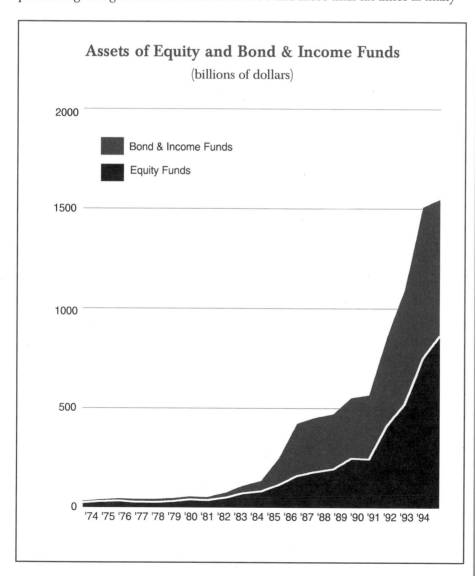

Assets of Equity and Bond & Income Funds

(billions of dollars)

as yearend 1984. Since total industry accounts numbered 114.9 million, long-term funds represented 78 percent of all mutual fund shareholder accounts, a 3 percent higher share than in 1993.

Recent Trends in Activity: Taxable and Tax-exempt Money Market Funds

By the end of 1994, assets in short-term funds (taxable and tax-exempt money market funds) rose to $611 billion, compared with figures of $565.3 billion and $546.2 billion for the two preceding years.

For the third consecutive year, sales of taxable money market mutual funds (MMMFs) exceeded $2 trillion; but for the first time since 1983, they did not post record numbers. However, following a lull during the spring and summer months, taxable money market fund sales picked up late in 1994 as short-term interest rates continued to rise.

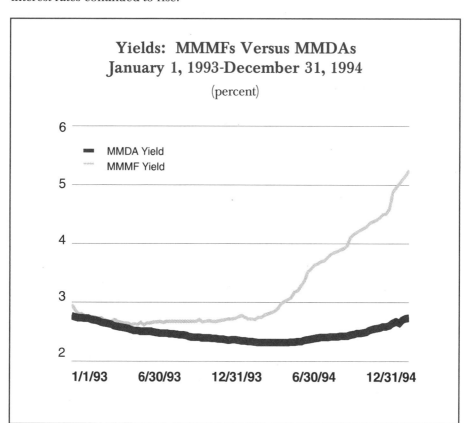

Yields: MMMFs Versus MMDAs
January 1, 1993-December 31, 1994
(percent)

Total sales of tax-exempt money market funds posted a new all-time high of $369.4 billion in 1994, 8 percent higher than the previous record of $341.9 billion in 1993. Tax-exempt money market fund assets grew to $110.6 billion, up 7 percent from the 1993 yearend total of $103.4 billion.

The average annual yield of taxable MMMFs in 1994 was 3.1 percent, which compared favorably with the 2.8 percent average in 1993. As a result, taxable money market funds remained popular among investors seeking relative safety and returns competitive with those of money market deposit accounts (MMDAs).

Investors typically use money market funds in three ways: for savings, cash management, and as a safe harbor between other investment transactions. As a cash management tool, money market funds allow investors to earn market rates on

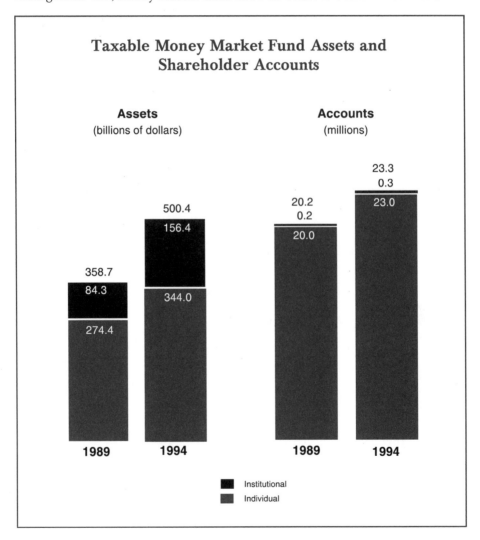

Taxable Money Market Fund Assets and Shareholder Accounts

assets used for paying everyday bills. (Institutions use money market funds this way on a larger scale.) As a result, money market funds have become an increasingly important tool in financial planning.

RETAIL VERSUS INSTITUTIONAL FUND ACCOUNTS

The two broad types of money market mutual funds, the individual and institutional varieties, respond to somewhat different investor needs. A money market fund primarily sold to individuals may also wind up servicing institutions as well. However, institutional money market funds typically aim at clients such as corporations and bank trust departments, and in the interests of maintaining lower expenses and larger account sizes, rarely include individuals.

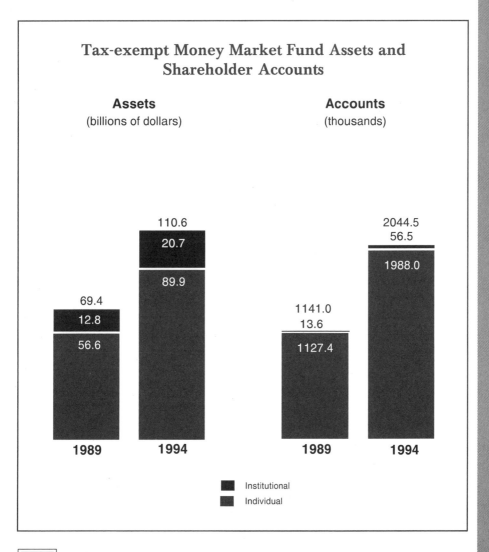

Tax-exempt Money Market Fund Assets and Shareholder Accounts

Assets
(billions of dollars)

Accounts
(thousands)

Institutional
Individual

Of the $500.4 billion in taxable money market fund assets held at the close of 1994, institutional funds held $156.4 billion, or 31 percent, down from a 35 percent portion in 1993. Taxable money market funds geared toward individuals held the remaining $344 billion. Of the $110.6 billion in tax-exempt money market fund assets, institutional funds held $20.7 billion, or 19 percent; individual-oriented funds accounted for $89.9 billion.

The number of shareholder accounts in taxable money market mutual funds stood at 23.3 million at yearend 1994. Individual-oriented funds represented 99 percent of those accounts, while institutional funds serviced the remaining 263,145. Tax-exempt money market fund accounts totaled roughly two million at yearend 1994, with 97 percent attributable to individual-oriented funds.

Institutional Markets

Outstanding investment performance, diversification, and other services are among the many reasons why institutions, in addition to individuals, have enthusiastically embraced mutual funds. Increasingly, retirement plan sponsors, foundations, nonprofit organizations, personal trusts and estates, and corporations have turned to mutual funds as investment options. As the accompanying chart shows, the value of institutional assets under management rose to $897.6 billion at the end of 1994.

Over the past several years, institutional assets have accounted for an increasing share of total mutual fund assets. At the end of 1994, more than 41.6 percent of all mutual fund assets were held by institutions, a slight increase from the 40.5 percent level reached at yearend 1993.

Institutional assets represented 47.5 percent of total money market fund assets at the end of 1994, reflecting the ongoing popularity of short-term taxable and tax-exempt investment options. Institutional assets in money market funds rose to

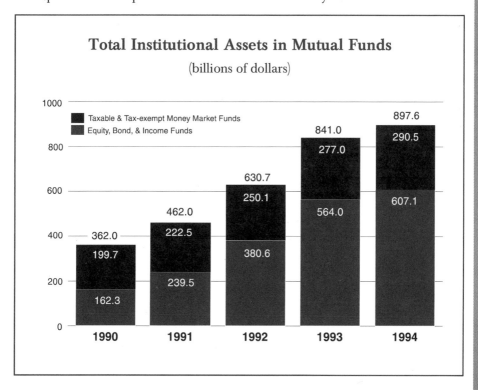

CHAPTER 12

Total Institutional Assets in Mutual Funds
(billions of dollars)

Taxable & Tax-exempt Money Market Funds
Equity, Bond, & Income Funds

Year	1990	1991	1992	1993	1994
Total	362.0	462.0	630.7	841.0	897.6
Money Market Funds	199.7	222.5	250.1	277.0	290.5
Equity, Bond, & Income Funds	162.3	239.5	380.6	564.0	607.1

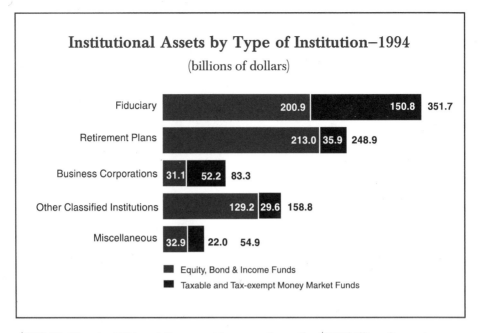

Institutional Assets by Type of Institution–1994
(billions of dollars)

	Equity, Bond & Income Funds	Taxable and Tax-exempt Money Market Funds	Total
Fiduciary	200.9	150.8	351.7
Retirement Plans	213.0	35.9	248.9
Business Corporations	31.1	52.2	83.3
Other Classified Institutions	129.2	29.6	158.8
Miscellaneous	32.9	22.0	54.9

■ Equity, Bond & Income Funds
■ Taxable and Tax-exempt Money Market Funds

$290.5 billion in 1994, a 4.9 percent increase from the $277 billion figure in 1993. Institutional assets in stock and bond and income funds grew to $607.1 billion, up from $564 billion at yearend 1993.

Along with the rise in assets, the number of institutional accounts also expanded. At the end of 1994, institutional accounts totaled 18.3 million, compared with 14.3 million in 1993. Since many of these are pooled accounts, the number of fund customers linked to institutions is considered even larger.

The institutional marketplace is complex and each of its submarkets has many unique characteristics. By far, the largest such market is the fiduciary group, which represents nearly 54.1 percent of all institutional accounts and 39.2 percent of all institutional assets. The fiduciary market comprises at least two broad segments: bank trusts and individuals serving as trustees, guardians, and administrators. Money market funds mainly serve the former market, while the longer-term funds primarily serve the latter. As a result, the average money market fund fiduciary account is much larger than the typical longer-term fiduciary account.

By yearend 1994, fiduciary fund accounts of all types numbered 10 million, almost 30.4 percent higher than at yearend 1993. The total value of fiduciary accounts also rose: as of December 31, 1994, they had an estimated total value of $351.7 billion, 8.1 percent more than their yearend 1993 value of $325.3 billion.

Other statistics relating to the institutional market can be found in the *Fact Book* data section, beginning on page 134.

Mutual Funds: A Global Marketing Perspective

In recent years, the mutual fund industry has become an important financial force in the global arena—even in smaller, less developed countries with emerging market economies.

As nations have moved to open their markets, introducing efficiencies such as privatization and reducing trade barriers, investment opportunities have proliferated. Consequently, investors in all countries are beginning to focus more attention abroad to take advantage of the growth and diversification potential.

In just the last five years, available data indicates that worldwide assets in mutual funds have grown from $2.11 trillion to $4.48 trillion. In that same span, investment company assets in 20 countries (those for which a complete series of data exists) grew 94.4 percent, or at an average annual compound rate of 14.2 percent. Much of the growth was in the U.S. market, which grew at a 17.1 percent average annual compound rate. In the 19 other countries, growth was slower but still impressive, increasing at an 11.5 percent average annual compound rate.

Because investors throughout the world share the same basic needs and goals, such as a comfortable retirement, education for their children, and improved living standards, it is not surprising that mutual funds have flourished on a global scale. Indeed, in many countries, individuals now show a preference for mutual funds over other forms of investments.

The expectation for continually growing middle classes in many industrialized and emerging markets is expected to lead to even greater global expansion of mutual fund sales. Furthermore, as the wealth of this population sector continues to expand, so, too, should the markets for mutual funds.

U.S. FUNDS LOOK ABROAD

U.S. mutual fund management companies target investors in foreign countries as well. The two most common routes to expanding globally are selling existing U.S. funds abroad or setting up new foreign funds in foreign markets. The former strategy, however, with limited exceptions, can be difficult to accomplish. Many U.S. investment management companies choose the second route, establishing separate foreign management subsidiaries in local markets to sponsor and advise foreign funds. As a result, fund sponsors can tailor funds to meet the customs, regulatory, and taxation requirements of a particular country, all of which can benefit the fund's investors.

THE VARIOUS FOREIGN MARKETS

Europe. The markets of Europe have generated much interest from U.S. mutual fund managers in recent years. Europe had begun to create a single mutual fund market when a European Community (EC) Directive known as the Undertakings for Collective Investment in Transferable Securities (UCITS) was implemented in October 1989, and generated much interest from U.S. investors.

The UCITS Directive facilitated cross-border marketing of mutual fund shares in EC countries, permitting registered funds in one EC country to offer shares more easily in other European countries. (Recent attempts to facilitate cross-border marketing of money market funds, however, has not generated as much success in Europe. To date, members of the European Union (EU), which replaced the EC, have failed to reach agreement on proposals to include money market funds under the UCITS Directive.)

Besides facilitating cross-border marketing, UCITS also established a common regulatory scheme regarding investment policies, public disclosure, structure, and control. Specifically, UCITS introduces the principle that host-country regulation of marketing and advertising cannot discriminate against funds of another EU country.

UCITS does not address common tax treatment or marketing practices, and each country retains authority over the marketing of any mutual fund shares. And while there may be no legal prohibitions against a foreign fund marketing shares in a particular jurisdiction, de facto barriers of custom and administrative practice can impede a foreign fund's access to EU markets.

To function within the UCITS framework, mutual fund managers must register new funds within the borders of an EU nation that has enacted appropriate UCITS legislation. Generally, some fund administrative functions must also be located within one of those jurisdictions. Once registered, the fund manager must then seek appropriate distribution channels in any countries selected for marketing.

Europe contains some of the most affluent and financially sophisticated markets in the world, and includes approximately 400 million consumers. Aggregate mutual fund assets in Europe totaled more than $1.581 trillion in 1994, up 15 percent from 1993, and represented 35 percent of the world share.

Judging by 1994 statistics, the EU should not be considered a homogeneous market, however. For example, close to 70 percent of assets in the German mutual fund industry (public funds only) were concentrated in fixed-income mutual funds, and shares were sold primarily through banks. France, the EU's largest

Assets of Open-end Investment Companies
(millions of U.S. dollars)

	1989	1990	1991	1992	1993	1994
NON-USA COUNTRIES						
Australia*	$30,892	$29,125	$34,543	$19,280	$24,556	$44,050
Austria	12,750	14,324	15,079	15,029	18,174	23,464(b)
Belgium	5,027	4,538	6,067	8,954	15,149	19,725(b)
Canada*	20,270	21,483	43,195	52,921	86,567	97,631(b)
Denmark	3,820	3,614	3,729	3,658	4,401	5,406(b)
Finland	N/A	N/A	77	110	N/A	1,155(b)
France	295,750	378,826	429,556	447,338	483,327	531,085(b)
Germany Public	62,352	71,018	77,266	70,196	78,552	93,101(b)
Special	62,189	74,477	88,942	101,405	133,734	160,335(b)
Greece	132	936	952	1,018	3,465	6,111(b)
Hong Kong	N/A	N/A	N/A	16,351	31,135	32,540(b)
India	5,957(d)	7,645(d)	7,895(d)	5,835(d)	7,925	11,033(b)
Ireland(a)	6,715	6,977	7,452	5,905	5,244	7,056(b)
Italy	38,700	41,924	48,823	41,036	64,272	86,344(b)
Japan	408,165	353,528	323,913	346,924	454,608	466,892(b)
Korea	27,584	33,806	37,050	49,183	69,988	78,190(b)
Luxembourg	N/A	94,559	117,112	182,244	247,804	289,033(b)
Netherlands*	23,204	24,308	21,340	34,797	48,530	49,306(b)
New Zealand*	N/A	N/A	N/A	1,062	1,833	2,397(b)
Norway	N/A	N/A	N/A	2,722	N/A	5,214(b)
Portugal	1,308	2,848	6,380	7,925	9,319	11,711(b)
South Africa	N/A	N/A	N/A	4,524	4,647	6,855(b)
Spain	7,927	11,996	40,025	54,699	72,058	90,175(b)
Sweden	23,739	21,113	20,779	18,108	24,356	26,465(b)
Switzerland	N/A	N/A	N/A	24,304	34,094	39,941(b)
United Kingdom(c)	92,850	91,530	104,394	91,153	131,455	135,197(b)
TOTAL NON-USA	**1,129,331**	**1,288,575**	**1,434,569**	**1,606,681**	**2,055,193**	**2,320,412**
USA (long-term)	553,862	568,517	853,000	1,100,100	1,510,100	1,550,400
(short-term)	428,093	498,375	542,500	546,200	565,300	611,000
TOTAL USA	**981,955**	**1,066,892**	**1,395,500**	**1,646,300**	**2,075,400**	**2,161,400**
TOTAL WORLD	**$2,111,286**	**$2,355,467**	**$2,830,069**	**$3,252,981**	**$4,130,593**	**$4,481,812**

a=Approximately 95% relates to life assurance-linked fund; the other 5% are unit investment trusts. International Financial Service Center funds are not included. b=As of September, 1994. c=Fund-of-fund assets not included. d=As of June 30.

Note: Comparison of annual total assets across countries is not recommended because reporting coverage, dates, and definitions are not consistent.

*Includes real estate funds

mutual fund investor, devoted more than one half of assets to money market funds and more than 28 percent to fixed-income funds. The Italian market employs more distribution channels than either France or Germany: for example, fund shares were often sold through banks, but investors also utilized sales networks.

The industry in the United Kingdom closely resembles that of the U.S.; as such, U.K. distribution channels varied more widely than those in the rest of the EU. Independent intermediaries captured 29 percent of all U.K. unit trust (mutual fund) sales and 50 percent of retail unit trust sales in 1994; the remaining fund sales came from company representatives. The U.K. has more stock funds than other European markets, with more than 91 percent of its unit trust industry invested in equity offerings, suggesting a higher risk tolerance in this marketplace.

Canada and Mexico. Canada is an attractive market for U.S. fund managers for a number of reasons, including proximity, modest language barriers, similar fund structure, and tax incentives. By yearend 1994, the Canadian fund industry had assets totaling $97.6 billion (in U.S. dollars), more than 46 percent of which was invested in equity mutual funds.

Certain Canadian jurisdictions, such as Ontario, recently began permitting U.S. investment advisers to register within their borders. U.S. money managers that register as advisers in Canada can organize and sponsor mutual funds for sale there. Distribution is a concern, however, because fund companies generally must sell their products through the highly competitive Canadian independent distribution network.

Under the North American Free Trade Agreement (NAFTA), which took effect in late 1993, opportunities increased in Mexico because U.S. firms could establish wholly-owned mutual fund operating companies that sponsor, advise, and distribute Mexican mutual funds. It is also expected that Mexican mutual funds will be able to invest more easily in foreign securities as a result of NAFTA's passage.

With regard to emerging markets such as Mexico, fund managers must weigh the benefits of growth and diversification potential against the different risks that securities in these markets present.

Investments in emerging markets can be more volatile than those found in the historically more stable markets. Unstable political, social, or economic conditions are more likely to occur in emerging market countries, such as those in Latin America, Eastern Europe, or the Far East than in more established nations, such as the U.S. and those in Western Europe.

Finally, foreign investing of any kind involves currency risk, whereby an investor can experience a gain or loss merely through exchanges in and out of a foreign currency.

The Pacific Rim.   Another promising market for U.S. mutual fund managers is the Pacific Rim. In this diverse market, mutual fund companies need extensive research to understand the regulatory environment as well as the marketing opportunities and limitations.

Despite recent economic difficulties, Japan remains attractive to mutual funds because of the country's economic status, the outstanding savings rate of its people, and the large accumulation of mutual fund assets there ($466.9 billion at yearend 1994).

As 1995 began, the U.S. and Japan had entered into a trade agreement that should open the Japanese pension and mutual fund markets to U.S. firms. As a practical matter, the Japanese securities markets still present imposing barriers to U.S. financial services firms, but the new pact represents an important step toward affording American firms increased access to the promising Japanese pension and mutual fund markets.

EXTENDED WORLDWIDE NEGOTIATIONS IN 1995

When negotiations concluded on the General Agreement on Tariffs and Trade (GATT) in late 1993, no final worldwide agreement had been reached concerning liberalization of trade barriers in financial markets. The parties involved in the GATT negotiations, including the United States, agreed to begin extended talks under the auspices of the World Trade Organization (WTO) to seek an agreement by July 1, 1995. The United States has reserved the right to modify its commitment to keep its financial services markets open if it is not satisfied with the results of the extended negotiations.

As the major differences in the regulatory schemes governing fund operations and marketing worldwide are overcome, however, the resulting cooperative global market is expected to benefit not only the mutual fund industry but the investors in all nations.

The Retirement Market: 401(k) Plans Become Popular

While much attention focuses on the unprecedented popularity of mutual funds, in general, the retirement plan market is one of, if not the most important, engines driving the industry's continued growth.

It seems that investors realize that many mutual funds match perfectly with the long-term objectives of investing for retirement, particularly in defined contribution plans such as 401(k) plans. By the end of 1993 (the latest data available), for example, the increasing investor preference for mutual funds as retirement plan vehicles was well documented:

■ Retirement plan assets, exclusive of variable annuities, accounted for 31 percent of industry assets.

■ Mutual funds held $110.1 billion, or 23.2 percent, of the $475 billion 401(k) market, quite a jump from the 14.8 percent share in 1992.

■ Mutual funds increased their share of the $245 billion Section 403(b) retirement plan market to $20.8 billion, a 53 percent increase in assets over 1992. Section 403(b) arrangements may cover only employees of public educational systems and other specific tax-exempt organizations (generally hospitals and other nonprofit groups).

■ Mutual funds held $9.8 billion of the $51 billion in Section 457 retirement plans. These plans are deferred compensation arrangements for government employees and employees of certain tax-exempt organizations.

By the end of 1994, similar trends were uncovered in other types of retirement plans:

■ Mutual funds held $285.3 billion, or 31.1 percent, of the $917 billion Individual Retirement Account (IRA) market.

■ The number of mutual fund IRA accounts stood at 31.1 million, up from 500,000 in 1981, the year when IRAs were liberalized to allow all working Americans to create do-it-yourself retirement programs.

Estimated Value of IRA Plans Outstanding–Yearend*

(billions of dollars)

	1989	1990	1991	1992	1993R	1994
Commercial Banks	$98.9	$118.6	$134.4	$136.9	$134.1	$133.1
Thrifts	97.5	94.9	91.1	85.3	76.6	73.7
Life Insurance Companies	37.8	42.0	49.7	55.6	69.5	75.0(pe)
Credit Unions	26.2	29.1	32.3	32.5	32.4	32.4
Mutual Funds	111.8	127.3	169.1	211.0	283.9	285.3
Self-directed**	82.0	117.1	180.6	224.7	271.0	317.5
TOTAL	**$454.2**	**$529.0**	**$657.2**	**$746.0**	**$867.5**	**$917.0**

Percent Distribution of IRA Assets–Yearend

(percent)

	1989	1990	1991	1992	1993R	1994
Commercial Banks	21.8%	22.5%	20.5%	18.4%	15.5%	14.5%
Thrifts	21.5	17.9	13.9	11.4	8.8	8.0
Life Insurance Companies	8.3	7.9	7.6	7.5	8.0	8.2
Credit Unions	5.8	5.5	4.9	4.4	3.7	3.5
Mutual Funds	24.6	24.1	25.7	28.3	32.7	31.1
Self-directed**	18.1	22.1	27.5	30.1	31.2	34.6
TOTAL	**100.0%**	**100.0%**	**100.0%**	**100.0%**	**100.0%**	**100.0%**

R = revised   pe = preliminary estimate

*Includes rollovers and Simplified Employee Pensions (SEPs).
**Includes only those self-directed items not included in other categories (including stocks, bonds, CDs sold by brokers, nonproprietary and other mutual funds not reported to ICI for the mutual fund category) and should not be misinterpreted as the total self-directed universe for IRAs. Also includes new reporters beginning in 1991 with assets of $23.4 billion, $22.7 billion, $23.4 billion, and $32.2 billion for 1991-1994.

Source: Federal Reserve Board, ACLI, CUNA, ICI special survey.

CHAPTER 14

■ Use of mutual funds in certain institutional retirement accounts (private trusteed pension assets) jumped to 7.3 percent, up from just 1.7 percent in 1984.

The statistics tell only part of the success story, however. Mutual funds make sense as long-term investment vehicles because of their intrinsic features, such as diversification and professional management. And because of the variety of funds available, retirement investors can select a mutual fund to meet nearly any long-term objective and risk/reward preference. Moreover, the exchange feature, which most mutual fund families provide, enables shareholders to adjust holdings among funds when economic conditions or personal financial situations change. Finally, many funds provide a wide range of other services, such as investor education, automatic payroll deduction plans, automatic withdrawal plans (for retirees), and complete recordkeeping.

*IRAs, rollovers, plans for the self-employed, and corporate plans
are the primary source of the mutual fund industry's retirement assets;
Section 403(b) and 457 plans also play a role.*

INDIVIDUAL RETIREMENT ACCOUNTS (IRAs)

Of all types of retirement vehicles, the IRA has rapidly claimed the largest share of the mutual fund industry's assets. Despite the volatile financial market environment of 1994, for example, mutual fund IRA assets (excluding street name accounts) grew by $1.4 billion, or one half of 1 percent. In 1993 and 1992, when financial markets were more favorable, asset growth was 35 and 25 percent, respectively; meanwhile the number of IRA mutual fund accounts increased by an average of 3.5 million over each of the past three years.

A longer-term perspective also illustrates the important role IRAs play in the mutual fund arena. At the end of 1981, the year that deductible IRAs were made available to all working Americans, IRA accounts comprised only 1.1 percent of mutual fund industry assets. By yearend 1994, that share of assets (excluding street name accounts) had grown to 13.2 percent. In addition, 27.1 percent of all mutual fund accounts at yearend 1994 were IRA accounts. (Note: Some IRA mutual fund shareholders hold multiple accounts.)

The mutual fund industry has also increased its market share of IRA assets. At the end of 1984, mutual funds comprised 12.8 percent of the total IRA universe; by the end of 1993, that share had grown to 32.7 percent, the largest for any financial product. With a 31.1 percent of market share at yearend 1994, the mutual fund industry was the second largest source of IRA assets behind self-directed accounts. Indeed, since self-directed accounts include nonproprietary mutual funds sold by brokers, mutual funds are the retirement vehicle of choice for more than one third of all IRA assets.

In other trends, IRA investor preference seems to have shifted more toward stocks in recent years. Of the mutual fund industry's $285.3 billion in IRA assets in 1994, 153.7 billion, or 53.9 percent were in equity funds. By comparison, in 1989, equity funds held 46.6 percent of industry IRA assets. Furthermore, of the 31.1 million mutual fund IRA accounts at yearend 1994, equity funds comprised the lion's share, or 17.6 million; bond and income funds held 6.7 million, and money market funds, 6.8 million.

RETIREMENT ROLLOVERS

Mutual funds are playing an increasingly important role in the rollover market. In a rollover, money is moved from a retirement plan to an IRA or other tax qualified plan. Rollovers often occur when people who change jobs are entitled to take all or a portion of their retirement plan assets with them in a lump-sum distribution. Rollovers can also occur from an existing IRA to another IRA.

Now more than ever, employees changing jobs should arrange with their employer to transfer any lump-sum retirement distributions directly into an IRA or

CHAPTER 14

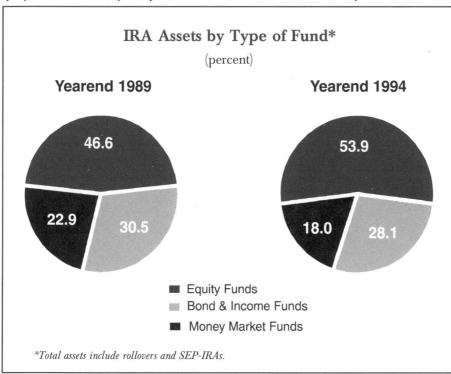

IRA Assets by Type of Fund*

(percent)

Yearend 1989   **Yearend 1994**

46.6   53.9

22.9   30.5   18.0   28.1

■ Equity Funds
■ Bond & Income Funds
■ Money Market Funds

Total assets include rollovers and SEP-IRAs.

another tax-qualified plan. Beginning in 1993, employers must withhold 20 percent of lump-sum distributions made directly to employees, even if the employees expect to roll the distribution into an IRA within the prescribed 60-day period. Furthermore, employees taking direct possession of IRA assets (while still planning to rollover the amount of cash received) may have to pay taxes and a penalty on the amount withheld by the employer. By instead arranging to have lump-sum distributions moved directly into an IRA or other tax-qualified retirement plan, individuals can preserve the full value of their retirement plan assets.

For mutual funds, retirement assets resulting from rollovers have been increasing relative to other types of retirement plan assets. The 20 percent withholding law is expected to generate further growth because it provides an even stronger incentive for employees to maintain retirement money in an IRA or other tax-deferred plan.

Mutual Fund IRAs by Investment Objective
(percent)

Investment Objective	Percent of Assets as of 12/31/94
Aggressive Growth	8.1%
Growth	15.0
Growth & Income	14.7
Precious Metals	0.5
International	4.4
Global-Equity	4.6
Income-Equity	6.6
Flexible Portfolio	2.8
Balanced	4.7
Income-Mixed	4.6
Income-Bond	2.3
U.S. Government Income	5.0
Ginnie Mae	2.9
Global Bond	0.6
Corporate Bond	2.0
High-yield Bond	3.2
Taxable Money Market	18.0

Growth in Mutual Fund IRA Plans

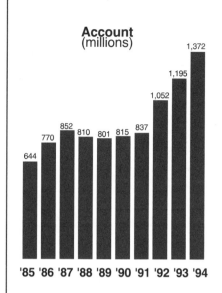

Account
(millions)

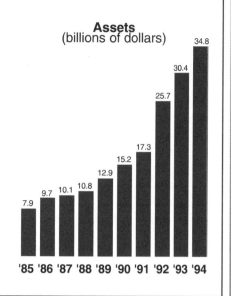

Assets
(billions of dollars)

Growth in Mutual Fund Self-employed Retirement Plans

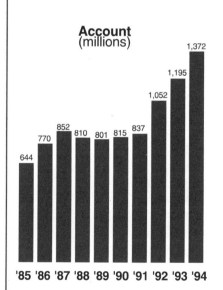

Account
(millions)

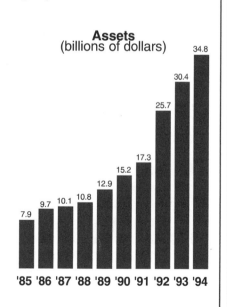

Assets
(billions of dollars)

RETIREMENT PLANS FOR THE SELF-EMPLOYED

The self-employed retirement plan market has been increasingly significant since the liberalization of tax laws in 1982. Although this change eliminated most distinctions between corporate plans and those maintained for the self-employed, certain restrictions apply to any plan which is a top-heavy plan, i.e., a plan under which a substantial portion of the benefits accrue on behalf of certain key employees of the employer. Most plans for the self-employed are treated as top-heavy plans subject to these restrictions. Many mutual fund complexes offer prototype top-heavy plans that comply with all of the new provisions of law.

In 1994, mutual fund retirement accounts for the self-employed numbered 1.4 million; assets for the same plans totaled $34.8 billion, up more than 14 percent from yearend 1993. Furthermore, 57 percent of the self-employed retirement plan assets managed by mutual funds were in equity funds, 23.4 percent in bond and income funds, and 19.6 percent in money market funds.

CORPORATE RETIREMENT PLANS

Since the 1970s, large and small companies alike have increasingly switched from defined benefit to defined contribution plans, such as 401(k) plans, to cut costs as well as shift control and responsibility for retirement funds to their employees. Not-for-profit organizations and governmental entities can also utilize defined contribution plans through Section 403(b) and Section 457 plans.

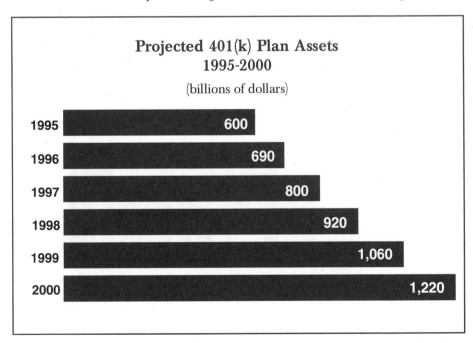

**Projected 401(k) Plan Assets
1995-2000**

(billions of dollars)

Year	Assets
1995	600
1996	690
1997	800
1998	920
1999	1,060
2000	1,220

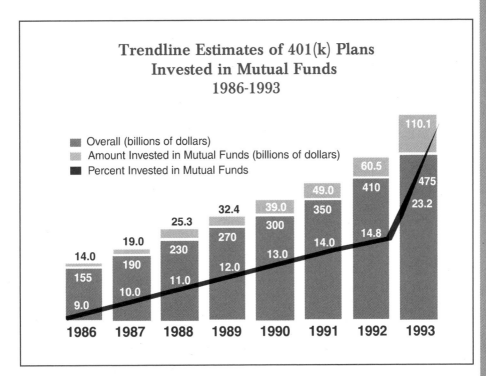

Trendline Estimates of 401(k) Plans Invested in Mutual Funds 1986-1993

Legend:
- Overall (billions of dollars)
- Amount Invested in Mutual Funds (billions of dollars)
- Percent Invested in Mutual Funds

Year	Overall	Amount Invested	Percent
1986	155	14.0	9.0
1987	190	19.0	10.0
1988	230	25.3	11.0
1989	270	32.4	12.0
1990	300	39.0	13.0
1991	350	49.0	14.0
1992	410	60.5	14.8
1993	475	110.1	23.2

The growth in defined contribution plans is evident when examining trends over the last few decades. In 1975, participants in defined benefit plans outnumbered those in defined contribution plans by 27.2 million to 11.2 million. By 1991, however, active participants in defined contribution plans (those with more than one participant) had grown to 36.3 million, compared with a decline to 26.1 million participants among defined benefit plans.

In 1983, defined contribution plan assets accounted for 31 percent of total private pension assets; by 1993, that share had grown to 44 percent, or $1.1 trillion. By the year 2000, defined contribution plan assets are projected to grow to 53 percent of total private pension assets, or about $2.3 trillion.

One of the most popular defined contribution plans is the 401(k) plan. Few large companies had 401(k) salary reduction plans ten years ago, but now most do. Indeed, many large companies added these plans to supplement defined benefit plans while small companies adoped them as primary plans in order to encourage employees to save more for retirement. The size of the 401(k) plan market is estimated to be $525 billion as of yearend 1994, up from $475 billion at yearend 1993.

The mutual fund industry's share of the 401(k) market has grown steadily each year since 1986. By yearend 1993, 401(k) assets in mutual funds jumped to more than $110 billion, or 23.2 percent, of the total 401(k) market; the $110 billion figure is also an 80 percent increase over the $61 billion invested in mutual fund 401(k) plans in 1992.

A study of major 401(k) market players revealed that the steep increase in mutual fund assets resulted from greater marketing efforts by fund companies as well as the conversion of some 401(k) plans from other insurance-company and commercial-bank products.

In recent years, mutual funds have made substantial progress attracting corporate retirement plan assets. Nearly 30 percent of mutual fund retirement assets is in defined contribution plans of private sector companies; more than half of that figure is in 401(k) plans.

Mutual funds are particularly well-suited to participant-directed defined contribution plans, like 401(k) plans, because they offer extensive choices to employees expected to take responsibility for their investment decisions. For years, mutual funds have been building the trust of investors through the use of service-oriented technology and shareholder communications. Fund companies have The Section 404(c) rules require plan sponsors to give participants sufficient information to allow them to make informed investment decisions. Unlike some investment vehicles, mutual funds are mandated by securities law to provide dis-

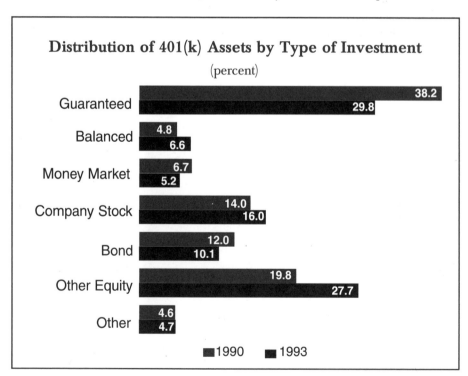

Distribution of 401(k) Assets by Type of Investment
(percent)

Type	1990	1993
Guaranteed	38.2	29.8
Balanced	4.8	6.6
Money Market	6.7	5.2
Company Stock	14.0	16.0
Bond	12.0	10.1
Other Equity	19.8	27.7
Other	4.6	4.7

■1990 ■1993

Retirement Plans

*Federal income tax laws permit the
establishment of a number of types of retirement plans,
each of which may be funded with mutual fund shares.*

Individual Retirement Accounts

All wage-earners under the age of 70 may set up an Individual Retirement Account (IRA). An individual may contribute as much as 100 percent of compensation each year, up to $2,000, and earnings are tax-deferred until withdrawal.

The amount contributed each year may be wholly or partially tax-deductible. Under the Tax Reform Act of 1986, all taxpayers not covered by employer-sponsored retirement plans can take the full deduction for IRA contributions. Those who are covered, or who are married to someone who is covered, must have an adjusted gross income of no more than $25,000 (single) or $40,000 (married, filing jointly) to take a full $2,000 deduction. The deduction is phased out for incomes between $25,000 and $35,000 (single) and $40,000 and $50,000 (married, filing jointly). An individual who qualifies for an IRA, and has a spouse who either has no earnings or elects to be treated as having no earnings, may contribute up to 100 percent of his or her income or $2,250, whichever is less.

Simplified Employee Pensions (SEPs)

SEPs are employer-sponsored plans that may be viewed as an aggregation of separate IRAs. In a SEP, the employer contributes up to $30,000 or 15 percent of compensation, whichever is less, to an Individual Retirement Account maintained for the employee. Effective in 1994, only $150,000 of compensation can be taken into account; therefore, the actual maximum contribution is $22,500.

SEPs established for employers with 25 or fewer employees may contain a cash or deferred arrangement allowing employees to make additional elective salary deferrals to the SEP. The cash or deferred arrangement for smaller employers is called a SARSEP, for salary reduction SEP.

Corporate and Self-employed Retirement Plans

Tax-qualified retirement and profit-sharing plans may be established by corporations or self-employed individuals. Changes in the tax laws have made retirement plans for employees of corporations and those for self-employed individuals essentially comparable. Contributions to a plan are tax-deductible and earnings accumulate on a tax-sheltered basis.

The maximum annual amount that may be contributed to a defined contribution plan on behalf of an individual is generally limited to the lesser of 25 percent of the individual's compensation or $30,000.

Section 403(b) Plans

Section 403(b) of the Internal Revenue Code permits employees of certain tax-exempt organizations and public educational systems to establish tax-sheltered retirement programs. These plans may be invested in either annuity contracts or mutual fund shares.

Section 401(k) Plans

One particularly popular type of tax-qualified retirement plan that may be offered by either corporate or noncorporate entities corporate or noncorporate entities is the 401(k) plan. A 401(k) plan is usually a profit-sharing plan that includes a cash or deferred arrangment. The cash or deferred arrangement permits employees to have a portion of their compensation contributed to a tax-sheltered plan on their behalf or paid to them directly as additional taxable complemension. Thus, an employee may elect to reduce his or her taxable compensation with contributions to a 401(k) plan where those amounts will accumulate tax-free. Employers often match these amounts with employer contributions. The Tax Reform Act of 1986 established new, tighter antidiscrimination requirements for 401(k) plans and curtailed the amount of elective deferrals that may be made by all employees. The recent GATT legislation would also limit COLAs (cost-of-living adjustments) for 401(k) plans beginning in 1995. Nevertheless, 401(k) plans remain excellent and popular retirement savings vehicles.

also developed the tools necessary for educating plan participants about investing for retirement, as well as the asset allocation services that can assist in directing participant accounts.

In 1992, the Department of Labor issued new defined contribution plan rules that are expected to further the growth of 401(k), profit-sharing, and other retirement plans. Under the Employee Retirement Income Security Act (ERISA) Section 404(c), plan sponsors can achieve a measure of relief from fiduciary liability in managing defined contribution plans for employees if they offer their employees adequate choices among types of investment categories.

Mutual funds assist plan sponsors in meeting the Section 404(c) requirements. For example, the rules call for sponsors to offer employees at least three investments with wide-ranging risk and return characteristics. Many fund organizations offer a complete family of funds representing different investment categories. As a result, plan sponsors can easily offer stock, bond & income, and money market funds. Section 404(c) rules also instruct plan sponsors to offer participants the opportunity to shift from one investment to another at least once every three months. Mutual funds offer daily pricing and an exchange feature whereby shareholders can move investments from one fund or funds to others within a family, or even to a different mutual fund group, depending on the plan's design.

closure documents such as prospectuses and annual reports. In addition, most major daily newspapers carry fund share prices, enabling participants to track their investments easily.

Retirement plan sponsors have come to appreciate the advantages mutual funds offer: professional money management, investment diversification, well-defined investment objectives and policies, documented track records, liquidity, and convenient administration. In turn, the mutual fund industry has shifted increasing attention toward retirement-oriented programs. As a result, the retirement market should prove to be a key source of sustainable growth for the mutual fund industry in the years ahead, and mutual funds should continue to be a key component in the retirement plans of millions of Americans.

Who Owns Mutual Funds?

An estimated 30.2 million U.S. households, or 31 percent, owned mutual funds in 1994. This estimate comprised households that owned money market, stock, and bond and income mutual funds, including those invested in 401(k), IRA, and Keogh accounts.

A 1992 survey of households owning mutual funds outside an employer-sponsored retirement plan found the "typical" mutual fund shareholder was middle-aged, married, and employed. The median age of a mutual fund shareholder was 46—more than ten years higher than that of the U.S. population as a whole. Seventy-two percent of mutual fund shareholders were married. Half of all fund shareholders completed four or more years of college, compared with 21 percent of all adults aged 25 and over. Shareholders' median household income was $50,000.

The typical shareholder household had financial assets of $114,000 at the time of the survey, excluding real estate and holdings in employer-sponsored retirement

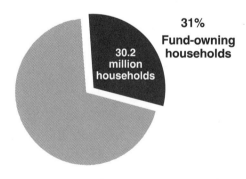

Ownership of Mutual Funds*
Among U.S. Households, 1994

(percent of U.S. households)

31%
Fund-owning
households

30.2
million
households

* Comprises ownership of money market, stock, bond and income funds, including those invested in IRA, Keogh, and 401(k) accounts.

Demographic Characteristics of Mutual Fund Shareholders, 1992*

Median age	46
Median household income	$50,000
Percent	
Male	56%
Four-year college degree or more	50
Married	72
Employed (full or part-time)	72
Retired from lifetime occupation	24
Spouse employed (full or part-time)**	68

*Shareholder refers to the household's primary financial decisionmaker or codecisionmaker for mutual fund investments.
**Percentage of married shareholders

Mutual Fund Ownership Charactersitics, 1992

(for households owning mutual funds)

Median number per household	
Mutual funds owned	2
Mutual fund companies with which fund assets are invested	2
Percent of households owning:*	
Equity mutual funds	72%
Bond and income mutual funds	41
Money market mutual funds	50

*Multiple responses included

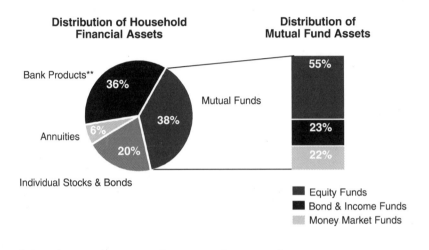

CHAPTER 15

Financial Characteristics of Mutual Fund Shareholders, 1992

(average per household)

Total Financial Assets* = $114,000
Financial Assets in Mutual Funds = $43,500

Distribution of Household Financial Assets

Bank Products** 36%

Annuities 6%

Individual Stocks & Bonds 20%

Mutual Funds 38%

Distribution of Mutual Fund Assets

55%

23%

22%

■ Equity Funds
■ Bond & Income Funds
□ Money Market Funds

*Excludes real estate and assets in employer-sponsored retirement plans.
**Includes passbook savings accounts, certificates of deposit, and money market deposit accounts.

plans. Mutual fund shares accounted for 38 percent, or $43,500, of these financial assets. Long-term funds–stock and bond and income funds–represented more than three quarters of the typical shareholder household's mutual fund holdings.

Shareholder households owned a median of two mutual funds from two mutual fund companies at the time of the survey. In addition, 48 percent of all shareholder households owned at least two of the three basic types of mutual funds (equity, bond and income, and money market funds). Equity funds were the most popular type of fund, with 72 percent of shareholders owning them. Half of all shareholders owned money market funds, and 41 percent owned bond and income funds.

First-time Buyers of Mutual Funds

Mutual funds have become a popular investment option in the last decade, and each year a segment of households makes its first fund purchase.

To understand how and why fund owners make that initial buying decision, the Investment Company Institute conducted a telephone survey in April 1994 of shareholders who purchased their first mutual fund between January 1992 and April 1994. To be included in the survey, a first-time buyer was (a) the household's primary or cofinancial decisionmaker for savings and investments, and (b) the decisionmaker who made the initial fund investment. Shareholders owning only funds purchased through their employers, such as in 401(k) plans, were excluded.

The survey found that first-time mutual fund buyers spanned all age groups. Thirty-seven percent were under 40, 47 percent were 40 to 64, and 16 percent were 65 and older.

Age of First-time Buyers

(percent of respondents)

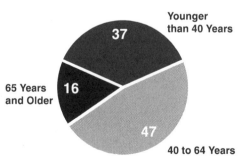

Note: First-time buyers are shareholders who purchased their first fund between January 1992 and April 1994.

FIRST-TIME BUYERS UNDER AGE 40

At the time of the survey, first-time buyers under 40 had a median household income of $47,000 and median household financial assets of $23,000; more than half were male and at least three fifths were college graduates.

More than three quarters of first-time buyers under 40 initially purchased an equity fund, and most used a full-service broker or bought directly from a fund company. Very few were introduced to funds through a bank, insurance agent, financial planner, or discount broker.

First-time buyers under 40 initially invested a median of $1,900 in mutual funds. As of April 1994, they had invested a median of $5,000 in funds and owned a median of two funds. Furthermore, mutual fund investments typically represented 22 percent of household financial assets.

FIRST-TIME BUYERS AGED 40 TO 64

Like first-time buyers under 40, those from 40 to 64 had a median household income of $47,000. However, these middle-aged first-time buyers had median household financial assets of $51,000, more than double that of their younger

First-time Buyer Characteristics by Age

	Younger than 40 Years	40 to 64 Years	65 Years and Older
Median			
Household income	$47,000	$47,000	$28,000
Household financial assets*	$23,000	$51,000	$57,000
Percent			
Male	51%	43%	36%
Married	67	64	45
Widowed	1	8	36
College degree or post-graduate	62	46	31
Employed full or part-time	90	80	14
Retired from lifetime occupation	1	15	85

*excludes primary residence and assets in employer-sponsored pension plans
Note: First-time buyers are shareholders who purchased their first fund between January 1992 and April 1994.

First-time Buyers' Initial Mutual Fund Purchase by Age

	Younger than 40 Years	40 to 64 Years	65 Years and Older
Median purchase amount	$1,900	$4,800	$8,500
Percent			
Type of fund purchased:			
Equity fund	77%	62%	45%
Taxable bond fund	3	9	18
Tax-exempt bond fund	8	18	31
Money market fund	12	10	5
Not specified	-	1	1
Distribution channel used:			
Sales force (net)	55	55	50
Full-service broker	28	29	38
Financial planner	15	16	11
Insurance agent	11	10	2
Direct market (net)	37	31	25
Fund company	33	29	22
Discount broker	4	3	3
Bank	7	13	25

Note: First-time buyers are shareholders who purchased their first fund between January 1992 and April 1994.

counterparts. Most first-time buyers aged 40 to 64 were female, married, and employed; 46 percent were college graduates.

Middle-aged first-time buyers' use of distribution channels for initial fund purchases and for the type of fund initially purchased approximated that of first-time buyers under age 40. First-time buyers from 40 to 64 made a median initial fund investment of $4,800. At the time of the survey, middle-aged first-time buyers had invested a median of $15,000 in mutual funds, which represented 29 percent of household financial assets.

FIRST-TIME BUYERS AGED 65 AND OLDER

First-time buyers aged 65 and older had a median household income of $28,000 and median household financial assets of $57,000. While most first-time buyers under 65 were employed at the time of the survey, most aged 65 and older were

First time Buyers' Fund Ownership
by Age
(medians)

	Younger than 40 Years	40 to 64 Years	65 Years and Older
Mutual fund assets	$5,000	$15,000	$19,000
Percent of financial assets invested in funds	22%	29%	33%
Numbers of funds owned	2	2	1

First-time buyers are shareholders who purchased thier first fund between January 1992 and April 1994. Fund ownership characteristics as of April, 1994

retired. Like seniors across the nation, most first-time buyers aged 65 and older had no college degrees.

Although the vast majority of first-time buyers under age 65 initially purchased equity fund shares, those 65 and older purchased a wider range of funds. Less than half of the senior first-time buyers initially purchased equity funds, approximately 30 percent bought tax-exempt bond fund shares, and about 20 percent purchased taxable bond fund shares. Compared with first-time buyers under 65, those 65 and older more often used a full-service broker or a bank for initial purchases. At the time of the survey, they had invested a median of $19,000 in mutual funds, or 33 percent of household financial assets.

Understanding Shareholder Choices of Ditribution Channels

Not only do mutual fund investors face a wide variety of choices when buying shares, but they must also weigh the benefits of a variety of distribution channels. Broadly speaking, shares may be purchased from a full-service broker, a discount broker, a bank, an insurance company, a financial planner, or the mutual fund company itself.

An analysis of recent buyers of long-term funds found that these shareholders used all six distribution channels, but with varying frequency. More than half of respondents owned funds purchased from the full-service broker channel and more than half owned funds from the direct market channel. Less than a fifth owned funds bought from each of the remaining channels: financial planner, discount broker, insurance, and bank.

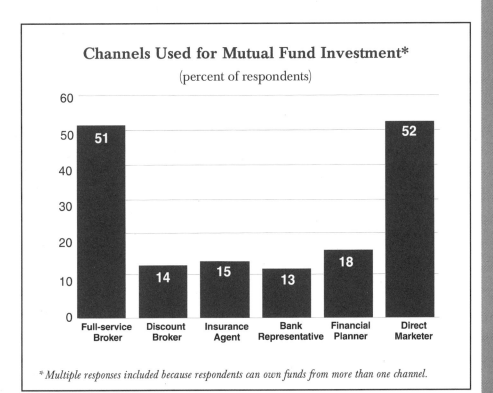

Channels Used for Mutual Fund Investment*

(percent of respondents)

* Multiple responses included because respondents can own funds from more than one channel.

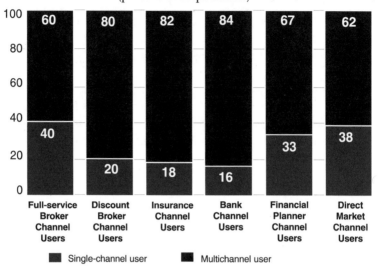

Use of Single and Multiple Channels

(percent of respondents)

	Full-service Broker Channel Users	Discount Broker Channel Users	Insurance Channel Users	Bank Channel Users	Financial Planner Channel Users	Direct Market Channel Users
Multichannel user	60	80	82	84	67	62
Single-channel user	40	20	18	16	33	38

■ Single-channel user   ■ Multichannel user

Note: Channel users are respondents who currently own at least one fund from that channel.

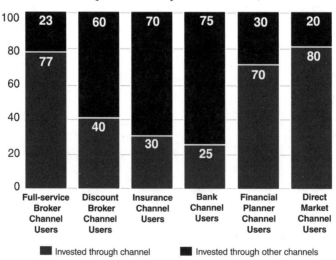

Distribution of Mutual Fund Assets

(percent of respondents' assets)

	Full-service Broker Channel Users	Discount Broker Channel Users	Insurance Channel Users	Bank Channel Users	Financial Planner Channel Users	Direct Market Channel Users
Invested through other channels	23	60	70	75	30	20
Invested through channel	77	40	30	25	70	80

■ Invested through channel   ■ Invested through other channels

Note: Channel users are respondents who currently own at least one fund from that channel.

Most of the respondents used more than one channel to purchase the funds they owned at the time of the survey. However, those respondents using the discount broker, insurance, and bank channels were more likely to be multichannel users than were those utilizing the full-service broker, financial planner, and direct market channels. In fact, four fifths or more of those in the former categories owned funds from at least one other channel. Two thirds or less of those using the latter categories owned funds from at least one other channel.

The research also found that respondents varied in their allocations to particular channels. Users of the full-service broker, financial planner, and direct market channels typically invested the majority of their mutual fund assets through these channels; those using the discount broker, bank, and insurance channels generally invested the majority of their mutual fund assets in other channels.

The need for advice, established relationships, low fees and commissions, and convenience were the most important factors determining an individual's choice of a distribution channel. Those respondents using a full-service broker or finan-

Primary Reason for Using Channels to Purchase Mutual Funds

(top three most frequently cited reasons)

	Full-service Broker Channel Users	Discount Broker Channel Users	Insurance Channel Users	Bank Channel Users	Financial Planner Channel Users	Direct Market Channel Users
Offers initial and ongoing investment advice or guidance	1		2		1	
Has low or no fees or commissions		1				1
Have an established relationship with adviser or institution	2		1	2	2	
Offers funds with solid performance						2
Is a convenient way to purchase an investment		2	3	1		3
Offers personalized service	3			3	3	
Executes orders efficiently		3				

Note: Channel users are respondents who currently own at least one fund from that channel.

cial planner most often cited advice and guidance as their key reason for using these channels. Low fees and commissions primarily attracted respondents to the discount broker and direct market channels. Bank channel users most often cited convenience, and insurance channel users pointed to their established relationship with an adviser or institution.

Glossary of Mutual Fund Terms

For an explanation of fund types, see pages 17-18; for retirement plans, see pages 77-78.

Advisor. *An organization employed by a mutual fund to give professional advice on the fund's investments and asset management practices (also called the investment adviser).*

Annual and Semiannual Reports. *Summaries that a mutual fund sends to its shareholders, which discuss the fund's performance over a defined period and identify the securities currently in the fund's portfolio.*

Asked or Offering Price. *(as seen in some mutual fund newspaper listings). The price at which a mutual fund's shares can be purchased. The asked or offering price includes the current net asset value per share plus any sales charge.*

Assets. *The investment holdings and cash owned by a mutual fund.*

Automatic Reinvestment. *A shareholder-authorized purchase of additional shares using dividends and capital gain distributions.*

Bear Market. *A period during which security prices are generally falling.*

Bid or Sell Price *(as seen in some mutual fund newspaper listings). The price at which a mutual fund's shares are redeemed, or bought back, by the fund. The bid or redemption price is usually the current net asset value per share.*

Blue Sky Laws. *A body of state laws governing registration and distribution of mutual fund shares. All 50 states and the District of Columbia regulate mutual funds.*

Bond. *A debt security issued by a company, municipality, or government agency. A bond investor lends money to the issuer and, in exchange, the issuer promises to repay the loan amount on a specified maturity date; the issuer also must pay the bondholder periodic fixed-interest payments over the life of the loan.*

Broker/Dealer (or Dealer). *A firm that buys and sells mutual fund shares and other securities from and to investors.*

Bull Market. *A period during which security prices are generally rising.*

Capital Appreciation. *An increase in the market value of a mutual fund's securities, as reflected in the net asset value of the fund's shares. Capital appreciation (or growth) is a specific long-term objective of many mutual funds.*

Capital Depreciation. *A decline in an investment's value.*

Capital Gain Distribution. *A payment to shareholders of profits realized when a security or securities in a mutual fund's investment portfolio are sold. A fund usually distributes capital gains to shareholders once a year, typically in December. For tax purposes, these profits may be considered short- or long-term gains and, therefore, incur different tax rates.*

Classes of Shares (e.g., Class A, Class B, etc.). *The growing trend among some fund organizations to provide multiple purchase options to investors. Multiple classes represent ownership in the same portfolio of securities, but permit shareholders to choose the type of fee structure that best suits their particular needs. For example, Class A shares of a fund might require payment of a front-end sales load, while Class B shares of the same fund might impose a contingent deferred sales charge and an annual 12b-1 fee instead of a front-end load. A fund's Class C shares might have annual 12b-1 and service fees, but no front-end or contingent deferred sales charge. Other classes of shares might be available to institutional investors only.*

Closed-end Investment Company. *Unlike a mutual fund, known as an open-end investment company, a closed-end investment company issues a limited number of shares that trade on a stock exchange or in the over-the-counter markets. The value of closed-end funds' shares is determined by market supply and demand.*

Commission. *A fee paid by an investor to a broker or other sales agent for investment advice and assistance.*

Compounding. *Earnings on an investment's earnings. For example, if you invest $1,000 at a fixed rate of 5 percent per year, your initial investment is worth $1,050 after one year. During the second year, assuming the same rate of return, earnings are based not on the original $1,000 investment, but also on the $50 in first-year earnings. Over time, compounding can produce significant growth in the value of an investment.*

Contingent Deferred Sales Charge (CDSC). *A fee imposed when shares are redeemed (sold back to the fund) during the first few years of share ownership.*

Contractual Plan. *A program for the accumulation of mutual fund shares in which an investor agrees to invest a fixed amount on a regular basis for a specified number of years.*

A substantial portion of any investment sales charge is usually deducted from early payments.

Custodian. *An organization, usually a bank, that holds the securities and other assets of a mutual fund.*

Direct Marketing. *A method of distribution whereby a fund company sells shares directly to the public without the intervention of a salesperson. Investors purchase fund shares through the mail or by telephone in response to advertising or other direct solicitations.*

Distribution. *1) The payment of dividends and capital gains, or 2) a term used to describe a method of selling to the public.*

Diversification. *The practice of investing broadly across a number of securities to reduce risk; a hallmark of mutual fund investing.*

Dollar-cost Averaging. *The practice of investing equal amounts of money at regular intervals, regardless of whether the securities markets are declining or rising. Hypothetically, this investment strategy reduces the average share cost to an investor, whose constant purchases acquire more shares as a security's price drops, and fewer as the price rises.*

Exchange Privilege. *The option enabling mutual fund shareholders to transfer their investment from one fund to another within the same fund family as their needs or objectives change. Typically, fund companies allow the use of the exchange privilege several times a year for a low fee or at no charge.*

Exdividend Date. *With regard to mutual funds, this is the day on which declared distributions (dividends or capital gains) are deducted from the fund's assets before it calculates its net asset value (NAV). The NAV per share will drop by the amount of the distribution per share.*

Expense Ratio. *A fund's cost of doing business—disclosed in the prospectus—as a percent of its assets.*

Family of Funds. *A group of mutual funds, each typically with its own investment objective, managed and distributed by the same company.*

Income. *Dividends, interest, and/or short-term capital gains paid to a mutual fund's shareholders. Income is earned on a fund's investment portfolio after deducting operating expenses.*

Investment Company. *A corporation, trust, or partnership that invests pooled shareholder dollars in securities appropriate to the organization's objective. Among the benefits of investment companies, compared to direct investments, are professional management and* *diversification. Mutual funds, also known as "open-end" investment companies, are the most popular type of investment company.*

Investment Objective. *The goal—long-term capital growth or current income, for example—that an investor and mutual fund pursue together. (See pages 17-18 for explanations of different objectives.)*

Long-term Funds. *An industry designation for all funds other than short-term funds (taxable and tax-exempt money market funds). Long-term funds are broadly divided into equity (stock) and bond and income funds.*

Liquidity. *The ability to redeem (sell back) all or a part of your mutual fund shares on any business day and receive the current value (which may be more or less than the original cost).*

Management Fee. *The amount paid by a mutual fund to the investment adviser for its services; the industrywide average annual fee is about one half of 1 percent of fund assets.*

Mutual Fund. *An investment company that pools money from shareholders and invests in a variety of securities, including stocks, bonds, and money market instruments. A mutual fund stands ready to buy back (redeem) its shares at their current net asset value, which depends on the total market value of the fund's investment portfolio at the time of redemption. As open-end investments, most mutual funds continuously offer new shares to investors.*

National Association of Securities Dealers, Inc. (NASD). *A self-regulatory organization with authority over firms that distribute mutual fund shares as well as other securities.*

Net Asset Value Per Share (NAV). *The market worth of one share of a mutual fund, this figure is calculated by adding a fund's total assets (securities, cash, and any accrued earnings), subtracting liabilities, and dividing by the number of shares outstanding.*

No-load Fund. *A mutual fund whose shares are sold at net asset value, i.e., without any sales charge.*

Open-end Investment Company. *The statutory terminology for a mutual fund, indicating that it stands ready to redeem (buy back) its unlimited number of shares on investor demand.*

Operating Expenses. *Normal business costs paid from a fund's assets before earnings are distributed to shareholders. A mutual fund incurs operating expenses as a result of employing staff; maintaining offices and equipment; and investing the fund's portfolio of securities.*

Over-the-Counter Market. *The universe of securities, both stocks and bonds, not listed on national or regional exchanges (such as the New York Stock Exchange or the Nasdaq Stock Market). Over-the-counter transactions are primarily conducted through an informal network or by auction.*

Payroll Deduction Plan. *An arrangement that some employers offer employees to accumulate mutual fund shares. Employees authorize their employer to deduct a specified amount from their salary at stated times and transfer the proceeds to the fund.*

Pooling. *The basic concept behind mutual funds in which a fund aggregates the assets of investors who share common financial goals. A fund uses the investment pool to buy a diversified portfolio of investments, and each mutual fund share purchased represents ownership in all the fund's underlying securities.*

Portfolio. *A collection of securities owned by an individual or an institution (such as a mutual fund) that may include stocks, bonds, and money market securities.*

Portfolio Managers. *Specialists employed by a mutual fund company to invest its pool of assets in accordance with predetermined investment objectives.*

Portfolio Turnover. *A measure of the trading activity in a fund's investment portfolio; in essence, how often securities are bought and sold by a fund.*

Principal. *The basic amount of money you invest, not to be confused with reinvested dividends or capital gains.*

Professional Management. *The full-time, experienced team of professionals that decides what securities to buy, hold, and sell for a mutual fund portfolio.*

Prospectus. *The official document that describes a mutual fund to all prospective investors. The prospectus contains information required by the Securities and Exchange Commission, such as investment objectives and policies, services, and fees.*

Redeem. *To cash in shares by selling them back to a mutual fund company. Mutual fund shares may be redeemed on any business day.*

Redemption Price. *The amount per share (shown as the "bid" in newspaper tables) that mutual fund shareholders receive when they cash in shares. The value of a fund's shares on any given day depends on the market value of its underlying investment portfolio at that time.*

Reinvestment Privilege. *An option whereby mutual fund dividends and capital gain distributions automatically buy new fund shares and thus increase the investor's holdings.*

Risk. *The possibility that an investment may fluctuate in value. Such factors as credit quality, currency exchange rates, inflation rates, or the direction of interest rates may increase an investment's volatility. The level of risk incurred by a shareholder varies from fund to fund. (See risk/reward tradeoff.)*

Risk/Reward Tradeoff. *The investment principle that an investment must offer higher potential returns as compensation for the likelihood of increased volatility. Investors normally accept higher risk on long-term investments, where the effects of price volatility usually diminish over time; they generally seek lower risk on short-term investments, where accessibility and preservation of principal override the need for maximum return.*

Rollover. *The shifting of an investor's assets from one qualified retirement plan to another—due to changing jobs, for instance—without a tax penalty.*

Sales Charge or Load. *The amount charged for fund shares sold by brokers or other sales professionals. By regulation, a mutual fund sales charge may not exceed 8.5 percent of an investment purchase, although the charge may vary depending on the amount invested and the fund chosen. A sales charge or load is reflected in the asked or offering price (see Asked or Offering Price).*

Sales Force Marketing. *A distribution method in which fund shares are sold to the public through sales professionals such as brokers, financial planners, and insurance agents. Some fund companies sell shares directly to the public through their own sales professionals.*

Securities and Exchange Commission (SEC). *The primary U.S. federal agency regulating the registration and distribution of mutual fund shares.*

Series Funds. *Funds that are organized with separate portfolios of securities, each with its own investment objective.*

Shareholder. *An investor who owns shares of a mutual fund or other company.*

Short-term Funds. *An industry designation for mutual funds that invest primarily in securities maturing in periods of one year or less (i.e., money market funds); these include taxable and tax-exempt funds.*

Statement of Additional Information (SAI). *The supplementary document (to a prospectus) that contains updated or more detailed information about a mutual fund; also known as "Part B" of the registration statement.*

Stock. *A share of ownership or equity in a corporation. A corporation's financial performance chiefly determines the value of its stock.*

Total Return. *A measure that takes into account all three components of an investment's performance: dividends, capital gains, and price appreciation.*

Transfer Agent. *The organization employed by a mutual fund to prepare and maintain records relating to shareholder accounts; some fund companies serve as their own transfer agents.*

12b-1 Fee. *A mutual fund expense named for the SEC rule that describes it. These fees pay for distribution costs, such as advertising and commissions paid to dealers. Any 12b-1 fees will be included in the fee table of a fund's prospectus. Recent NASD rules placed two caps on the level of 12b-1 fees. One is an annual limit of 0.75 percent of a fund's assets. (An additional 0.25 percent service fee may be paid to brokers or other sales professionals in return for providing ongoing information and assistance.) The other is a rolling cap on total sales charges, to be calculated at 6.25 percent of new sales plus interest for funds that pay a service fee, and 7.25 percent plus interest for funds that do not pay a service fee.*

Underwriter. *The organization acting as the distributor of a mutual fund's shares to broker/dealers and investors.*

Unit Investment Trust. *An investment company that maintains a fixed portfolio of income-producing securities (i.e., the portfolio is not traded) with a specific maturity date; trust units are typically sold to investors by brokers.*

Variable Annuity. *An investment contract sold by an insurance company; capital is accumulated, often through mutual fund investments, and converted to an income stream later, often at an investor's retirement.*

Withdrawal Plan. *A program whereby shareholders receive income or principal payments from their mutual fund investments at regular intervals.*

Yield. *The income per share paid by a fund to its shareholder over a specified period of time. Yield is expressed as a percentage of the fund's current price per share. For example, if a fund distributed $1.00 per share during a year and, at the end of the year, its price was $20.00 per share, its yield would be 5 percent ($1/$20 = 5%).*

GLOSSARY

Data Section
Table of Contents

SECTION THREE: Short-term Funds
(Taxable and Tax-exempt Money Market Funds)

SECTION FOUR: Exchanges for All Funds

SECTION FIVE: Retirement Funds

SECTION SIX: Institutional Investors

Total Industry Net Assets

(billions of dollars)

Year	Equity Funds	Bond & Income Funds	Taxable Money Market Funds	Tax-exempt Money Market Funds	Total
1970	$45.1	$2.5	-	-	$47.6
1971	51.6	3.4	-	-	55.0
1972	55.9	3.9	-	-	59.8
1973	43.0	3.5	-	-	46.5
1974	30.9	3.2	$1.7	-	35.8
1975	37.5	4.7	3.7	-	45.9
1976	39.2	8.4	3.7	-	51.3
1977	34.0	11.0	3.9	-	48.9
1978	32.7	12.3	10.9	-	55.9
1979	35.9	13.1	45.2	$0.3	94.5
1980	44.4	14.0	74.5	1.9	134.8
1981	41.2	14.0	181.9	4.3	241.4
1982	53.7	23.2	206.6	13.2	296.7
1983	77.0	36.6	162.5	16.8	292.9
1984	83.1	54.0	209.7	23.8	370.6
1985	116.9	134.8	207.5	36.3	495.5
1986	161.5	262.6	228.3	63.8	716.2
1987	180.7	273.1	254.7	61.4	769.9
1988	194.8	277.5	272.3	65.7	810.3
1989	249.1	304.8	358.7	69.4	982.0
1990	245.8	322.7	414.7	83.6	1,066.8
1991	411.6	441.4	452.6	89.9	1,395.5
1992	522.8	577.3	451.4	94.8	1,646.3
1993	749.0	761.1	461.9	103.4	2,075.4
1994	866.5	684.0	500.4	110.6	2,161.5

Total Industry Shareholder Accounts

(millions)

Year	Equity Funds*	Bond & Income Funds	Taxable Money Market Funds	Tax-exempt Money Market Funds	Total
1978	6.8	1.4	0.5	-	8.7
1979	6.1	1.4	2.3	-	9.8
1980	5.8	1.5	4.8	-	12.1
1981	5.7	1.5	10.3	-	17.5
1982	6.2	2.0	13.1	0.1	21.4
1983	9.2	2.8	12.3	0.3	24.6
1984	10.0	4.4	13.6	0.3	28.3
1985	11.5	8.3	14.4	0.5	34.7
1986	16.6	13.2	15.6	0.7	46.1
1987	21.4	15.5	16.8	0.8	54.5
1988	20.6	15.6	17.6	0.9	54.7
1989	21.5	15.4	20.2	1.1	58.2
1990	23.0	16.6	21.6	1.4	62.6
1991	26.1	18.9	21.9	1.7	68.6
1992	33.2	23.4	21.8	1.9	80.3
1993	42.5R	27.5R	21.6	2.0	93.6R
1994	59.1	30.5	23.3	2.0	114.9

*Equity funds could not be counted separately from bond & income funds before 1978.

Total Number of Funds

Year	Equity Funds	Bond & Income Funds	Taxable Money Market Funds	Tax-exempt Money Market Funds	Total
1978	294	150	61	-	505
1979	289	159	76	-	524
1980	288	170	96	10	564
1981	306	180	159	20	665
1982	340	199	281	37	857
1983	396	257	307	66	1,026
1984	471	349	326	95	1,241
1985	579	492	346	111	1,528
1986	701	654	359	126	1,840
1987	846	930	388	153	2,317
1988	1,016	1,094	431	174	2,715
1989	1,080	1,173	463	201	2,917
1990	1,127	1,235	508	235	3,105
1991	1,217	1,389	554	267	3,427
1992	1,356	1,629	586	279	3,850
1993	1,615	2,023	628	292	4,558
1994	1,944	2,450	644	319	5,357

An Overview:
Shareholder Accounts,
Total Net Assets, and Liquid Assets
Equity and Bond & Income Funds
1970-1994

Calendar Yearend	Number of Reporting Funds	Number of Accounts (thousands)	Net Assets (billions of dollars)	Liquid Assets (billions of dollars)
1970	361	10,690.3	$47.6	$3.1
1971	392	10,901.0	55.0	2.6
1972	410	10,635.3	59.8	2.6
1973	421	10,330.9	46.5	3.4
1974	416	9,970.4	34.1	3.4
1975	390	9,667.3	42.2	3.2
1976	404	8,879.4	47.6	2.4
1977	427	8,515.1	45.0	3.3
1978	444	8,190.6	45.0	4.5
1979	446	7,482.2	49.0	4.7
1980	458	7,325.5	58.4	5.3
1981	486	7,175.5	55.2	5.3
1982	539	8,190.3	76.9	6.0
1983	653	12,065.0	113.6	8.3
1984	820	14,423.6	137.1	12.2
1985	1,071	19,845.6	251.7	20.6
1986	1,355	29,790.2	424.1	30.7
1987	1,776	36,855.0	453.8	38.0
1988	2,110	36,212.0	472.3	45.1
1989	2,253	36,968.3	553.9	44.8
1990	2,362	39,614.0	568.5	48.6
1991	2,606	44,974.4	853.1	60.8
1992	2,985	56,567.8R	1,100.1	74.4
1993	3,638	70,049.2R	1,510.1	100.2
1994	4,394	89,557.0	1,550.5	121.3

Note: Figures for shareholder accounts represent combined totals for member companies. Duplications have not been eliminated.

R = Revised
Comparable data for short-term funds can be found on page 123.
Industry totals can be found on pages 101-102

Type of Shareholder Accounts
Equity and Bond & Income Funds
1973-1994

Yearend	Total Shareholder Accounts	Regular Accounts	Contractual Accumulation Plans	Contractual Single Payment Plans	Withdrawal Accounts
Number (thousands)					
1973	10,331	8,699	1,214	166	252
1974	9,970	8,524	1,081	140	225
1975	9,667	8,302	1,029	126	210
1976	8,879	7,647	930	112	190
1977	8,515	7,395	844	101	175
1978	8,191	7,203	757	75	156
1979	7,482	6,602	677	64	139
1980	7,326	6,598	554	45	129
1981	7,175	6,486	537	30	122
1982	8,190	7,573	471	28	118
1983	12,065	11,326	585	20	134
1984	14,424	13,666	615	17	126
1985	19,846	19,010	647	17	172
1986	29,790	28,919	624	16	231
1987	36,855	35,887	687	17	264
1988	36,212	35,331	605	16	260
1989	36,968	36,108	561	14	285
1990	39,614	38,769	463	4	378
1991	44,974	44,112R	497R	15	350
1992	56,568R	56,218	107	1	242R
1993	70,049R	69,340R	131	0	578R
1994	89,557	88,661	301	0	595
Percent					
1973	100.0%	84.2%	11.8%	1.6%	2.4%
1974	100.0	85.5	10.8	1.4	2.3
1975	100.0	85.9	10.6	1.3	2.2
1976	100.0	86.1	10.5	1.3	2.1
1977	100.0	86.9	9.9	1.2	2.0
1978	100.0	87.9	9.3	0.9	1.9
1979	100.0	88.2	9.0	0.9	1.9
1980	100.0	90.1	7.6	0.6	1.7
1981	100.0	90.4	7.5	0.4	1.7
1982	100.0	92.5	5.8	0.3	1.4
1983	100.0	93.8	4.9	0.2	1.1
1984	100.0	94.8	4.2	0.1	0.9
1985	100.0	95.8	3.2	0.1	0.9
1986	100.0	97.0	2.1	0.1	0.8
1987	100.0	97.4	1.8	0.1	0.7
1988	100.0	97.6	1.7	0.0	0.7
1989	100.0	97.7	1.5	0.0	0.8
1990	100.0	97.8	1.2	0.0	1.0
1991	100.0	98.1	1.1	0.0	0.8
1992	100.0	99.4	0.2	0.0	0.4
1993	100.0	99.0	0.2	0.0	0.8
1994	100.0	99.0	0.3	0.0	0.7

R = Revised

Total Net Assets of Equity and Bond & Income Funds by Fund Characteristics
Yearend
(millions of dollars)

	1993		1994	
	Dollars	Percent	Dollars	Percent
Total Net Assets	**$1,510,047.3**	**100.0%**	**$1,550,490.4**	**100.0%**
Method of Sales				
Sales Force	$876,474.4	58.0%	$878,546.1	56.6%
Direct Marketing	487,811.4	32.3	505,324.0	32.6
Variable Annuity	144,566.6	9.6	165,492.6	10.7
Not Offering Shares	1,194.9	0.1	1,127.7	0.1
Investment Objective				
Aggressive Growth	$123,734.5	8.2%	$110,407.1	7.1%
Growth	167,145.2	11.1	228,761.2	14.8
Growth & Income	276,952.0	18.3	292,906.1	18.9
Precious Metals	5,564.6	0.4	5,237.8	0.3
International	71,024.8	4.7	101,744.6	6.6
Global Equity	43,269.7	2.9	60,175.6	3.9
Income-Equity	61,262.5	4.1	67,215.9	4.3
Flexible Portfolio	34,973.6	2.3	44,338.3	2.9
Balanced	58,031.2	3.8	59,209.6	3.8
Income-Mixed	53,934.3	3.6	57,939.5	3.7
Income-Bond	55,467.1	3.7	53,038.7	3.4
U.S. Government Income	116,448.7	7.7	86,950.4	5.6
Ginnie Mae	73,200.5	4.9	53,695.9	3.5
Global Bond	38,235.2	2.5	31,395.6	2.0
Corporate Bond	27,517.1	1.8	25,217.6	1.6
High-yield Bond	48,708.5	3.2	45,055.7	2.9
National Municipal Bond–Long-term	140,999.4	9.3	122,400.6	7.9
State Municipal Bond–Long-term	113,578.4	7.5	104,800.2	6.8

Liquid Assets of Equity and Bond & Income Funds by Fund Characteristics

Yearend

(millions of dollars)

	1993		1994	
	Dollars	Percent	Dollars	Percent
Total Liquid Assets	**$100,209.0**	**100.0%**	**$121,295.8**	**100.0%**
Method of Sales				
Sales Force	$50,510.2	50.4%	$63,544.7	52.4%
Direct Marketing	39,507.0	39.4	45,305.7	37.4
Variable Annuity	10,168.1	10.2	12,417.8	10.2
Not Offering Shares	23.7	0.0	27.6	0.0
Investment Objective				
Aggressive Growth	$10,323.3	10.3%	$10,195.0	8.4%
Growth	14,806.5	14.8	21,447.4	17.7
Growth & Income	16,781.6	16.7	17,152.5	14.1
Precious Metals	376.5	0.4	243.0	0.2
International	7,617.9	7.6	10,543.3	8.7
Global Equity	4,771.5	4.7	7,149.3	5.9
Income Equity	4,883.1	4.9	6,792.3	5.6
Flexible Portfolio	5,395.9	5.4	7,525.9	6.2
Balanced	6,477.8	6.5	6,961.8	5.7
Income Mixed	4,190.3	4.2	4,604.5	3.8
Income Bond	5,637.5	5.6	6,136.6	5.1
U.S. Government Income	1,122.1	1.1	2,412.9	2.0
Ginnie Mae	222.5	0.2	1,572.8	1.3
Global Bond	7,123.8	7.1	5,068.4	4.2
Corporate Bond	1,022.3	1.0	1,536.8	1.3
High-yield Bond	2,183.2	2.2	3,549.9	2.9
National Municipal Bond-Long Term	4,878.1	4.9	5,514.9	4.5
State Municipal Bond-Long Term	2,395.1	2.4	2,888.5	2.4

Liquid Asset Ratio–Equity Funds

	January	February	March	April	May	June	July	August	September	October	November	December
1968	6.4	8.2	9.4	8.7	7.4	7.0	6.6	7.2	7.5	6.8	6.4	6.2
1969	7.4	8.0	8.5	8.9	8.2	7.9	8.9	9.5	8.9	9.0	8.4	8.0
1970	7.6	7.5	7.3	7.9	8.8	9.9	10.3	9.8	9.0	8.6	7.9	6.6
1971	6.3	6.1	5.4	4.8	4.2	4.6	4.9	4.8	4.0	4.7	5.3	4.7
1972	4.7	5.1	4.7	4.1	3.9	4.4	4.8	4.9	5.0	5.5	5.0	4.2
1973	4.6	5.5	6.2	6.7	7.5	7.6	7.9	8.0	7.7	7.0	7.8	7.5
1974	8.0	8.4	8.6	8.9	9.1	9.3	9.8	10.9	11.8	10.7	10.7	10.1
1975	8.8	9.7	8.2	7.8	7.5	6.8	7.1	7.5	7.8	7.4	7.6	7.6
1976	6.0	5.5	5.1	4.8	5.2	4.8	4.6	4.7	4.5	4.5	5.0	4.9
1977	5.3	6.0	6.5	6.1	6.6	6.2	6.8	7.5	7.9	8.2	8.0	7.5
1978	8.5	10.2	10.3	10.1	9.5	9.2	8.0	6.9	6.5	6.7	7.9	8.2
1979	8.1	8.9	8.3	8.5	8.8	8.7	8.7	8.5	8.2	7.9	8.2	7.9
1980	8.5	9.0	9.2	9.5	10.4	10.1	10.4	10.3	9.8	9.7	9.3	9.1
1981	8.1	8.4	8.3	8.5	9.0	9.0	8.7	9.4	10.4	10.8	11.4	10.5
1982	10.5	10.4	10.8	10.5	11.4	12.2	11.0	10.1	9.2	8.9	8.4	8.6
1983	9.7	9.5	9.9	9.9	9.5	9.4	9.0	7.7	8.6	7.9	8.7	7.8
1984	8.0	8.5	9.1	9.4	9.3	9.7	10.1	9.5	9.3	8.8	9.1	9.2
1985	8.6	9.3	8.3	9.1	8.9	8.8	9.2	9.8	9.9	10.7	9.7	9.4
1986	9.6	8.6	9.1	9.9	9.5	9.2	9.8	9.6	10.1	9.7	9.5	9.6
1987	9.4	9.4	9.0	10.3	9.3	9.3	9.3	8.8	9.2	10.4	11.2	9.2
1988	10.1	9.9	10.3	10.8	10.5	10.1	10.6	10.6	10.6	10.0	9.7	9.4
1989	9.4	9.0	8.7	9.8	9.2	9.8	9.9	10.2	10.2	10.6	11.1	10.4
1990	11.5	11.6	11.9	12.5	11.3	10.8	10.7	11.9	12.7	12.9	12.4	11.5
1991	9.6	9.5	8.8	8.5	8.5	8.0	7.7	7.2	7.4	7.9	8.4	7.5
1992	7.2	7.3	7.8	8.3	8.1	8.8	8.8	9.1	8.5	8.5	8.7	8.2
1993	8.2	8.8	9.1	9.5	8.6	8.4	8.6	8.1	8.0	8.3	8.3	8.0
1994	8.3	8.9	8.1	8.2	8.6	8.4	8.8	8.4	8.4	8.5	9.0	8.5

Liquid Asset Ratio–Bond & Income Funds

	January	February	March	April	May	June	July	August	September	October	November	December
1968	4.7	8.6	7.1	6.1	5.7	4.0	5.9	6.5	5.2	3.9	3.5	3.7
1969	4.0	4.2	6.9	6.5	5.7	8.5	10.1	9.2	9.9	9.0	6.5	7.9
1970	7.1	6.8	6.1	6.2	6.2	7.4	6.8	7.2	6.5	8.9	6.8	5.5
1971	4.4	3.5	3.3	2.4	3.0	2.9	2.6	4.1	4.7	6.5	5.6	5.7
1972	5.2	5.2	5.3	4.4	4.6	5.2	5.9	6.0	6.8	6.1	5.8	5.9
1973	3.3	3.9	3.9	4.0	4.6	4.8	5.8	6.2	6.3	5.2	6.3	6.2
1974	6.0	6.3	6.7	7.0	7.4	7.5	8.2	9.4	9.9	8.5	8.3	7.8
1975	9.4	8.5	7.9	7.8	8.3	7.4	7.7	7.8	7.8	6.9	7.2	7.7
1976	6.4	6.4	6.1	6.0	5.7	5.4	5.5	5.6	5.7	5.2	4.8	5.0
1977	6.5	6.9	7.2	6.5	5.9	6.5	6.5	5.1	6.4	7.4	7.4	6.6
1978	8.7	8.9	8.3	8.6	10.4	11.6	11.5	10.6	10.8	13.4	14.4	14.8
1979	14.6	15.3	14.4	14.7	14.1	14.0	13.3	11.3	13.2	12.8	13.5	14.2
1980	16.0	16.7	17.3	15.4	11.5	8.9	10.1	9.6	9.9	9.7	8.4	9.3
1981	8.6	9.3	9.1	9.4	9.4	8.4	9.6	9.2	10.8	10.1	9.4	6.8
1982	8.5	10.7	10.9	11.8	9.8	10.3	10.8	8.8	7.7	7.2	6.9	6.2
1983	6.3	7.0	6.3	5.8	6.0	5.8	7.3	7.9	7.0	7.2	7.4	6.5
1984	7.5	7.9	9.0	9.2	10.6	11.5	10.1	10.6	11.8	8.5	8.0	8.5
1985	8.5	9.0	7.7	9.8	7.8	7.8	8.0	8.0	8.6	9.6	8.8	7.2
1986	7.5	7.7	7.9	7.6	7.1	6.8	6.3	5.8	6.2	6.2	5.5	5.8
1987	6.0	5.6	6.2	7.3	6.7	7.0	6.7	6.6	7.3	8.0	8.1	7.8
1988	7.5	7.7	8.5	8.7	9.0	8.2	8.3	9.1	9.3	9.2	9.0	9.6
1989	10.8	10.6	10.2	10.6	10.0	9.1	8.2	7.5	7.6	7.0	6.8	6.2
1990	7.3	7.7	6.9	8.2	7.4	5.8	6.4	7.1	7.2	7.2	7.3	6.3
1991	7.8	7.2	7.2	7.1	7.3	7.7	7.5	6.9	6.7	7.3	6.9	6.7
1992	7.2	7.2	6.7	6.7	6.4	6.1	6.1	6.7	6.8	6.5	6.5	5.4
1993	5.6	5.2	4.7	4.8	4.9	4.5	5.3	5.3	5.8	6.0	6.0	5.3
1994	5.6	5.7	6.8	7.4	7.0	6.7	6.6	6.3	6.8	7.2	7.0	7.0

Total Net Assets of Equity and Bond & Income Funds by Investment Objective Within Method of Sales—Yearend

(millions of dollars)

Sales Force

	1991	1992	1993	1994
Aggressive Growth	$16,097.3	$21,437.8	$35,555.5	$41,470.0
Growth	60,525.2	74,134.9	90,841.9	105,270.7
Growth & Income	78,950.1	102,259.4	130,045.4	141,152.2
Precious Metals	1,493.1	1,084.7	2,141.6	2,023.3
International	9,985.3	12,131.2	34,743.6	51,529.1
Global Equity	16,437.0	21,074.4	36,087.3	49,409.0
Income-Equity	14,267.3	20,330.8	30,140.2	28,528.0
Option/Income*	1,378.0	0.0	0.0	0.0
Flexible Portfolio	3,976.2	4,669.1	8,118.6	9,152.2
Balanced	9,698.7	14,259.7	23,716.4	22,814.3
Income-Mixed	20,225.8	26,407.7	40,072.3	45,974.9
Income-Bond	13,649.5	18,614.0	27,942.7	28,754.2
U.S. Government Income	82,089.6	99,452.3	92,911.3	73,268.0
Ginnie Mae	25,629.8	38,336.3	57,750.5	35,914.9
Global Bond	24,814.7	23,708.2	30,428.5	24,124.5
Corporate Bond	9,340.6	12,374.9	17,323.1	16,141.1
High-yield Bond	21,221.1	27,064.6	37,377.1	35,112.7
National Municipal Bond–Long-term	58,426.9	72,334.7	93,072.6	83,753.3
State Municipal Bond–Long-term	48,584.8	65,342.1	88,205.8	84,153.7
Total	**$516,791.0**	**$655,016.8**	**$876,474.4**	**$878,546.1**

Direct Marketing

	1991	1992	1993	1994
Aggressive Growth	$45,507.6	$58,538.9	$81,918.4	$59,335.0
Growth	34,303.5	46,344.6	59,945.3	102,823.5
Growth & Income	36,703.8	49,111.5	71,591.3	74,960.1
Precious Metals	1,357.9	1,038.0	3,332.9	3,079.0
International	8,523.9	9,854.4	32,802.5	43,635.3
Global Equity	609.1	1,487.1	4,411.1	5,247.0
Income-Equity	14,435.5	21,079.3	28,765.2	35,210.5
Option/Income*	0.0	0.0	0.0	0.0
Flexible Portfolio	2,385.8	5,214.1	12,333.1	16,904.0
Balanced	9,013.3	13,381.8	27,881.5	29,081.4
Income-Mixed	4,536.7	7,165.0	11,884.2	10,434.5
Income-Bond	10,925.0	17,464.2	20,988.1	18,077.4
U.S. Government Income	13,419.5	18,594.6	20,754.1	11,100.8
Ginnie Mae	11,169.4	13,723.3	14,306.0	16,717.9
Global Bond	2,338.6	7,616.0	6,717.7	5,290.8
Corporate Bond	5,476.0	6,703.9	8,608.1	7,538.6
High-yield Bond	3,977.5	5,688.8	8,272.5	6,594.4
National Municipal Bond–Long-term	29,923.0	38,511.7	47,926.8	38,647.3
State Municipal Bond–Long-term	17,267.1	20,070.8	25,372.6	20,646.5
Total	**$251,873.2**	**$341,588.0**	**$487,811.4**	**$505,324.0**

*As of January 1992, funds previously included in the Option/Income category were reclassified as Income-Equity funds.

Distribution of Mutual Fund Assets in
Equity and Bond & Income Funds
Yearend, 1976–1994

Year	Total Net Assets	Net Cash & Equivalent	Corporate Bonds	Preferred Stocks	Common Stocks	Municipal Bonds	Long-term U.S. Gov't	Other
Millions of dollars								
1976	$47,582	$2,352	$6,977	$655	$37,158	N/A	N/A	$440
1977	45,049	3,274	6,475	418	30,746	$2,256	$1,295	585
1978	44,980	4,507	5,545	405	30,678	2,550	1,093	202
1979	48,980	4,995	5,582	443	34,334	2,651	798	177
1980	58,400	5,321	6,582	531	41,561	2,866	1,433	106
1981	55,207	5,277	7,489	399	36,649	3,046	2,147	200
1982	76,841	6,040	10,833	1,628	47,720	6,797	3,752	71
1983	113,599	8,343	13,052	1,474	72,942	13,368	3,894	526
1984	137,126	11,978	15,018	1,627	81,597	18,522	8,009	375
1985	251,695	20,607	24,961	3,773	119,698	38,339	43,471	846
1986	424,156	30,716	47,310	7,387	153,657	70,875	111,536	2,675
1987	453,842	38,006	41,661	5,566	176,372	68,578	119,854	3,805
1988	472,297	45,090	54,441	5,678	173,684	86,136	103,750	3,518
1989	553,866	44,780	52,945	4,582	241,307	85,017	118,108	7,127
1990	568,517	48,324	44,344	2,843	216,605	118,820	128,485	9,096
1991	853,057	60,787	87,007	6,900	377,901	149,626	162,490	8,346
1992	1,100,065	74,381	115,991	10,573	479,328	191,619	225,341	2,832
1993	1,510,047	100,209	169,997	16,241	696,828	249,141	273,915	3,716
1994	1,550,490	121,296	157,189	16,498	812,681	210,349	222,147	10,330
Percent								
1976	100.0%	4.9%	14.7%	1.4%	78.1%	N/A	N/A	0.9%
1977	100.0	7.3	14.4	0.9	68.2	5.0%	2.9%	1.3
1978	100.0	10.0	12.3	0.9	68.2	5.7	2.4	0.5
1979	100.0	10.2	11.4	0.9	70.1	5.4	1.6	0.4
1980	100.0	9.1	11.3	0.9	71.2	4.9	2.4	0.2
1981	100.0	9.5	13.6	0.7	66.4	5.5	3.9	0.4
1982	100.0	7.9	14.1	2.1	62.1	8.8	4.9	0.1
1983	100.0	7.3	11.5	1.3	64.2	11.8	3.4	0.5
1984	100.0	8.7	11.0	1.2	59.5	13.5	5.8	0.3
1985	100.0	8.2	9.9	1.5	47.6	15.2	17.3	0.3
1986	100.0	7.3	11.2	1.7	36.2	16.7	26.3	0.6
1987	100.0	8.4	9.2	1.2	38.9	15.1	26.4	0.8
1988	100.0	9.5	11.5	1.2	36.8	18.2	22.0	0.8
1989	100.0	8.1	9.6	0.8	43.6	15.3	21.3	1.3
1990	100.0	8.5	7.8	0.5	38.1	20.9	22.6	1.6
1991	100.0	7.1	10.2	0.8	44.3	17.5	19.1	1.0
1992	100.0	6.8	10.5	1.0	43.6	17.4	20.4	0.3
1993	100.0	6.6	11.3	1.1	46.1	16.5	18.1	0.3
1994	100.0	7.8	10.1	1.1	52.4	13.6	14.3	0.7

N/A = Not Available

An Overview:
Sales, Redemptions, and Net Sales
of Equity and Bond & Income Funds
1970-1994

(millions of dollars)

Year	Sales	Redemptions	Net Sales
1970	$4,625.8	$2,987.6	$1,638.2
1971	5,147.2	4,750.2	397.0
1972	4,892.5	6,562.9	(1,670.4)
1973	4,359.3	5,651.1	(1,291.8)
1974	3,091.5	3,380.9	(289.4)
1975	3,307.2	3,686.3	(379.1)
1976	4,360.5	6,801.2	(2,440.7)
1977	6,399.6	6,026.0	373.6
1978	6,705.3	7,232.4	(527.1)
1979	6,826.1	8,005.0	(1,178.9)
1980	9,993.7	8,200.0	1,793.7
1981	9,710.4	7,470.4	2,240.0
1982	15,738.3	7,571.8	8,166.5
1983	40,325.1	14,677.6	25,647.5
1984	45,856.9	20,030.2	25,826.7
1985	114,313.5	33,763.4	80,550.1
1986	215,847.9	67,012.7	148,835.2
1987	190,628.0	116,224.3	74,403.7
1988	95,292.9	92,474.1	2,818.8
1989	125,711.0	91,655.5	34,055.5
1990	149,512.5	98,250.9	51,261.6
1991	236,633.3	116,325.3	120,308.0
1992	364,402.2	165,506.6	198,895.6
1993	511,578.5	231,356.2	280,222.3
1994	473,975.6	329,735.6	144,240.0

Comparable data for short-term funds can be found on page 123.

Sales of Equity and Bond & Income Funds
by Fund Characteristics
(millions of dollars)

	1993		1994	
	Dollars	Percent	Dollars	Percent
Total Sales	**$511,578.5**	**100.0%**	**$473,975.6**	**100.0%**
Method of Sales				
Sales Force	$290,463.7	56.8%	$243,221.7	51.3%
Direct Marketing	182,944.1	35.8	191,521.0	40.4
Variable Annuity	38,163.6	7.4	39,125.6	8.3
Not Offering Shares	7.1	0.0	107.3	0.0
Investment Objective				
Aggressive Growth	$39,974.9	7.8%	$53,093.5	11.2%
Growth	51,201.7	10.0	56,846.2	12.0
Growth & Income	71,247.9	13.9	66,150.6	14.0
Precious Metals	2,741.9	0.5	2,915.8	0.6
International	27,538.4	5.4	48,994.4	10.3
Global Equity	14,216.8	2.8	21,044.2	4.4
Income-Equity	21,891.6	4.3	21,721.6	4.6
Flexible Portfolio	12,142.5	2.4	16,210.4	3.4
Balanced	19,896.7	3.9	18,785.6	4.0
Income-Mixed	30,296.0	5.9	30,772.5	6.5
Income-Bond	27,801.4	5.4	24,469.5	5.2
U.S. Government Income	45,169.2	8.8	23,159.9	4.9
Ginnie Mae	27,534.3	5.4	9,927.5	2.1
Global Bond	19,031.2	3.7	12,441.4	2.6
Corporate Bond	9,863.9	1.9	6,917.9	1.5
High-yield Bond	16,659.3	3.3	14,291.8	3.0
National Municipal Bond–Long-term	41,427.7	8.1	26,283.3	5.5
State Municipal Bond–Long-term	32,943.1	6.5	19,949.5	4.2

Sales of Equity and Bond & Income Funds by Investment Objective Within Method of Sales–Yearend

(millions of dollars)

Sales Force	1991	1992	1993	1994
Aggressive Growth	$3,796.7	$6,711.6	$12,511.2	$16,219.3
Growth	13,937.5	20,469.8	25,910.0	28,670.8
Growth & Income	18,427.3	29,048.5	33,834.8	33,599.1
Precious Metals	169.3	138.5	576.3	539.0
International	2,653.3	3,883.5	12,643.3	24,184.5
Global Equity	2,438.3	3,446.7	10,946.4	15,941.2
Income-Equity	3,400.4	6,181.5	10,738.3	7,238.9
Option/Income*	164.2	0.0	0.0	0.0
Flexible Portfolio	771.9	1,844.9	2,234.1	2,466.9
Balanced	2,013.3	4,840.3	8,335.5	8,107.1
Income-Mixed	8,737.8	12,564.2	16,653.3	14,410.3
Income-Bond	4,786.2	7,906.0	13,847.1	12,233.3
U.S. Government Income	22,197.7	38,075.4	35,853.9	17,776.3
Ginnie Mae	9,782.6	22,172.6	22,869.7	7,275.2
Global Bond	14,122.4	9,347.0	14,057.5	8,309.5
Corporate Bond	2,472.4	3,610.2	5,481.3	4,018.9
High-yield Bond	4,529.9	8,034.7	11,991.8	9,953.7
National Municipal Bond–Long-term	13,125.5	18,995.6	26,579.2	16,968.8
State Municipal Bond–Long-term	13,050.7	17,356.0	25,400.0	15,308.9
Total	**$140,577.4**	**$214,627.0**	**$290,463.7**	**$243,221.7**

Direct Marketing	1991	1992	1993	1994
Aggressive Growth	$11,872.0	$15,539.9	$23,570.2	$31,342.6
Growth	9,038.2	15,510.8	18,757.1	21,639.8
Growth & Income	14,394.0	18,108.5	28,426.0	25,471.7
Precious Metals	1,415.0	603.7	2,033.8	2,109.0
International	3,710.8	4,747.3	12,717.7	21,161.2
Global Equity	236.8	704.6	2,290.5	2,977.0
Income-Equity	3,243.4	5,244.2	9,951.0	12,637.9
Option/Income*	0.0	0.0	0.0	0.0
Flexible Portfolio	640.8	2,193.8	6,565.7	9,830.3
Balanced	2,770.4	4,955.1	9,051.9	9,077.1
Income-Mixed	2,992.5	9,220.6	13,011.0	15,828.9
Income-Bond	4,664.1	7,087.9	11,164.4	10,436.1
U.S. Government Income	5,073.3	9,932.0	8,185.2	4,735.3
Ginnie Mae	4,166.6	5,198.2	4,262.0	2,409.7
Global Bond	1,405.0	4,388.4	4,231.5	3,283.7
Corporate Bond	2,399.4	3,941.4	3,624.6	2,237.0
High-yield Bond	1,137.8	2,196.5	2,710.0	2,388.6
National Municipal Bond–Long-term	7,959.4	11,871.1	14,848.4	9,314.5
State Municipal Bond–Long-term	5,477.1	6,670.1	7,543.1	4,640.6
Total	**$82,596.6**	**$128,114.1**	**$182,944.1**	**$191,521.0**

As of January 1992, funds previously included in the Option/Income category were reclassified as Income-Equity funds.

Sales and Reinvested Dividends by Fund Characteristics
1993-1994

(millions of dollars)

1993	Total Sales	Total Reinvested Dividends	Sales Less Reinvested Dividends
Total	**$511,578.5**	**$38,275.3**	**$473,303.2**
Method of Sales			
Sales Force	$290,463.7	$23,884.2	$266,579.5
Direct Marketing	182,944.1	12,107.6	170,836.6
Variable Annuity	38,163.6	2,278.4	35,885.1
Not Offering Shares	7.1	5.1	2.0
Investment Objective			
Aggressive Growth	$39,974.9	$1,219.7	$38,755.2
Growth	51,201.7	2,628.9	48,572.8
Growth & Income	71,247.9	5,862.2	65,385.7
Precious Metals	2,741.9	30.4	2,711.5
International	27,538.4	341.9	27,196.5
Global Equity	14,216.8	517.3	13,699.5
Income-Equity	21,891.6	1,833.9	20,057.8
Flexible Portfolio	12,142.5	542.4	11,600.1
Balanced	19,896.7	1,844.4	18,052.3
Income-Mixed	30,296.0	1,882.7	28,413.2
Income-Bond	27,801.4	2,329.9	25,471.5
U.S. Government Income	45,169.2	4,451.1	40,718.1
Ginnie Mae	27,534.3	2,265.5	25,268.8
Global Bond	19,031.2	1,402.8	17,628.4
Corporate Bond	9,863.9	1,165.7	8,698.1
High-yield Bond	16,659.3	2,319.0	14,340.3
National Municipal Bond–Long-term	41,427.7	4,516.3	36,911.4
State Municipal Bond–Long-term	32,943.1	3,121.2	29,822.0
1994			
Total	**$473,975.6**	**$39,355.9**	**$434,619.7**
Method of Sales			
Sales Force	$243,221.7	$24,654.1	$218,567.6
Direct Marketing	191,521.0	12,141.1	179,379.8
Variable Annuity	39,125.6	2,558.0	36,567.6
Not Offering Shares	107.3	2.7	104.7
Investment Objective			
Aggressive Growth	$53,093.5	$849.7	$52,243.8
Growth	56,846.2	2,184.7	54,661.5
Growth & Income	66,150.6	5,850.5	60,300.2
Precious Metals	2,915.8	63.9	2,851.9
International	48,994.4	1,277.7	47,716.6
Global Equity	21,044.2	796.5	20,247.7
Income-Equity	21,721.6	2,141.8	19,579.8
Flexible Portfolio	16,210.4	953.0	15,257.5
Balanced	18,785.6	1,997.7	16,787.9
Income-Mixed	30,772.5	2,101.3	28,671.1
Income-Bond	24,469.5	2,586.6	21,882.9
U.S. Government Income	23,159.9	3,631.5	19,528.4
Ginnie Mae	9,927.5	2,138.3	7,789.2
Global Bond	12,441.4	1,410.1	11,031.4
Corporate Bond	6,917.9	1,203.0	5,714.8
High-yield Bond	14,291.8	2,492.9	11,798.9
National Municipal Bond–Long-term	26,283.3	4,401.8	21,881.5
State Municipal Bond–Long-term	19,949.5	3,274.9	16,674.6

Equity and Bond & Income Funds'
Distributions to Shareholders
1970-1994

(millions of dollars)

| Year | Distributions from | |
	Net Investment Income	Net Realized Capital Gains
1970	$1,414.1	$922.1
1971	1,330.7	775.5
1972	1,286.6	1,402.6
1973	1,300.2	943.3
1974	1,553.2	484.3
1975	1,449.1	219.2
1976	1,580.0	470.9
1977	1,789.7	634.8
1978	2,116.0	710.6
1979	2,451.4	929.9
1980	2,669.0	1,774.2
1981	3,143.0	2,697.2
1982	3,832.9	2,350.1
1983	4,981.0	4,391.6
1984	7,238.4	6,019.2
1985	12,864.2	4,984.6
1986	22,273.4	17,463.8
1987	31,823.7	22,975.6
1988	31,978.3	6,345.3
1989	34,096.1	14,802.8
1990	32,917.7	8,054.6
1991	35,322.2	14,116.1
1992	59,177.0	22,335.6
1993	73,302.4	36,105.3
1994	61,517.3	29,969.6

Annual Redemption Rate
for Equity and Bond & Income Funds
1970-1994

(millions of dollars)

Year	Average Total Net Assets	Redemptions	Redemption Rate
1970	$47,954	$2,988	6.2%
1971	51,332	4,750	9.3
1972	57,438	6,563	11.4
1973	53,175	5,651	10.6
1974	40,290	3,381	8.4
1975	38,120	3,686	9.7
1976	44,880	6,801	15.2
1977	46,316	6,026	13.0
1978	45,014	7,232	16.1
1979	46,980	8,005	17.0
1980	53,690	8,200	15.3
1981	56,803	7,470	13.2
1982	66,024	7,572	11.5
1983	95,220	14,678	15.4
1984	125,362	20,030	16.0
1985	194,411	33,763	17.4
1986	337,926	67,013	19.8
1987	438,999	116,224	26.5
1988	463,070	92,474	20.0
1989	513,079	91,656	17.9
1990	561,189	98,251	17.5
1991	710,787	116,325	16.4
1992	976,561	165,507	16.9
1993	1,305,056	231,356	17.7
1994	1,530,269	329,736	21.5

Note: "Average Total Net Assets" are an average of values at the beginning of the year and at the end of the year. The redemption rate is the dollar redemption volume as a percent of average assets.

Redemptions of Equity and Bond & Income Funds by Fund Characteristics

(millions of dollars)

	1993		1994	
	Dollars	**Percent**	**Dollars**	**Percent**
Total Sales	**$231,356.2**	**100.0%**	**$329,735.6**	**100.0%**
Method of Sales				
Sales Force	$134,489.8	58.1%	$185,908.6	56.4%
Direct Marketing	86,971.0	37.6	127,093.3	38.5
Variable Annuity	9,835.3	4.3	16,665.7	5.1
Not Offering Shares	60.1	0.0	68.0	0.0
Investment Objective				
Aggressive Growth	$18,032.4	7.8%	$27,942.1	8.5%
Growth	24,861.4	10.8	33,086.5	10.0
Growth & Income	31,267.0	13.5	38,530.0	11.7
Precious Metals	1,847.0	0.8	2,564.2	0.8
International	6,789.3	2.9	21,417.2	6.5
Global Equity	3,485.6	1.5	7,212.8	2.2
Income-Equity	6,621.0	2.9	11,181.1	3.4
Flexible Portfolio	2,176.5	0.9	7,067.3	2.1
Balanced	4,837.0	2.1	10,431.1	3.2
Income-Mixed	14,903.9	6.4	19,448.8	5.9
Income-Bond	13,363.4	5.8	20,683.4	6.3
U.S. Government Income	30,496.5	13.2	35,276.7	10.7
Ginnie Mae	21,982.1	9.5	21,586.3	6.5
Global Bond	11,273.8	4.9	13,576.4	4.1
Corporate Bond	4,271.9	1.8	5,908.6	1.8
High-yield Bond	7,097.6	3.1	10,184.8	3.1
National Municipal Bond–Long-term	17,405.0	7.5	25,241.1	7.6
State Municipal Bond–Long-term	10,644.8	4.6	18,397.2	5.6

Redemptions of Equity and Bond & Income Funds by Investment Objective Within Method of Sales—Yearend

(millions of dollars)

Sales Force

	1991	1992	1993	1994
Aggressive Growth	$3,027.3	$3,051.8	$5,182.2	$7,904.5
Growth	7,038.6	8,684.6	13,233.2	16,701.2
Growth & Income	9,145.2	10,939.5	14,147.1	19,324.8
Precious Metals	311.0	222.8	411.1	453.7
International	1,455.8	1,799.6	2,882.5	9,193.3
Global Equity	2,005.1	1,996.7	2,668.3	4,974.0
Income-Equity	2,038.6	2,436.1	3,389.6	5,354.1
Option/Income	417.5	0.0	0.0	0.0
Flexible Portfolio	596.9	574.5	696.5	1,505.2
Balanced	975.4	1,411.2	2,205.7	5,010.7
Income-Mixed	4,682.0	4,447.6	5,345.5	8,002.8
Income-Bond	2,699.7	3,306.8	6,522.9	9,831.4
U.S. Government Income	14,121.9	21,582.8	25,479.0	29,333.1
Ginnie Mae	5,476.9	9,962.0	18,736.7	18,109.4
Global Bond	3,992.7	10,159.3	8,756.7	10,224.7
Corporate Bond	1,166.6	1,424.8	2,271.2	3,308.9
High-yield Bond	3,071.1	4,207.4	5,323.9	7,094.7
National Municipal Bond—Long-term	6,016.2	7,049.7	9,996.9	15,761.4
State Municipal Bond—Long-term	4,155.4	5,528.8	7,240.7	13,820.7
Total	**$72,393.9**	**$98,786.0**	**$134,489.7**	**$185,908.6**

Direct Marketing

	1991	1992	1993	1994
Aggressive Growth	$4,744.5	$7,223.3	$10,998.2	$17,544.8
Growth	4,323.0	5,453.8	9,446.0	13,813.5
Growth & Income	10,808.0	10,560.1	15,191.0	16,277.9
Precious Metals	1,279.7	515.1	1,361.6	1,937.7
International	1,600.6	2,283.1	3,626.0	11,277.8
Global Equity	177.0	273.0	714.4	1,765.0
Income-Equity	1,711.0	1,965.7	3,069.5	5,383.7
Option/Income	0.1	0.0	0.0	0.0
Flexible Portfolio	337.1	442.2	1,007.7	4,259.8
Balanced	746.0	1,057.4	2,299.3	4,788.4
Income-Mixed	1,898.9	7,128.2	9,450.8	11,201.9
Income-Bond	1,299.0	4,051.8	6,065.4	9,300.1
U.S. Government Income	1,513.1	3,650.1	4,684.3	5,186.9
Ginnie Mae	1,187.8	1,978.0	3,011.3	3,178.4
Global Bond	394.6	2,196.7	2,395.2	3,114.2
Corporate Bond	687.3	1,263.5	1,757.1	2,182.5
High-yield Bond	314.5	976.4	1,080.9	1,824.5
National Municipal Bond—Long-term	3,075.2	5,543.8	7,408.2	9,479.7
State Municipal Bond—Long-term	1,864.0	2,770.3	3,404.1	4,576.5
Total	$37,961.4	$59,332.5	$86,971.0	$127,093.3

As of January 1992, funds previously included in the Option/Income category were reclassified as Income-Equity funds.

Total Purchases, Total Sales, and Net Purchases
of Portfolio Securities by Mutual Funds
1970-1994

(millions of dollars)

Year	Total Purchases	Total Sales	Net Purchases
1970	$20,405.0	$18,588.5	$1,816.5
1971	25,360.2	24,793.8	566.4
1972	24,467.6	25,823.6	(1,356.0)
1973	19,706.6	21,903.0	(2,196.4)
1974	12,299.7	12,213.5	86.2
1975	15,396.9	15,511.4	(114.5)
1976	15,348.2	16,881.2	(1,533.0)
1977	18,168.0	19,420.7	(1,252.7)
1978	20,945.6	23,069.7	(2,124.1)
1979	22,412.1	23,702.5	(1,290.4)
1980	32,987.2	32,080.6	906.6
1981	36,161.7	33,709.2	2,452.5
1982	55,682.0	47,920.7	7,761.3
1983	93,009.5	71,466.5	21,543.0
1984	119,272.4	98,929.6	20,342.8
1985	259,578.5	186,974.6	72,603.9
1986	501,058.5	365,167.6	135,890.9
1987	531,075.8	485,640.1	45,435.7
1988	410,714.2	421,449.7	(10,735.5)
1989	472,218.6	445,730.4	26,488.2
1990	555,699.8	506,547.9	49,151.9
1991	736,771.8	608,908.4	127,863.4
1992	950,632.5	758,972.1	191,660.4
1993	1,337,057.0	1,061,038.5	276,018.5
1994	1,435,130.6	1,330,271.9	104,858.7

Note: Parentheses indicate net portfolio sales.

Total Purchases, Total Sales, and Net Purchases
of Common Stocks by Mutual Funds
1970-1994

(millions of dollars)

Year	Total Purchases	Total Sales	Net Purchases
1970	$17,127.6	$15,900.8	$1,226.8
1971	21,557.7	21,175.1	382.6
1972	20,943.5	22,552.8	(1,609.3)
1973	15,560.7	17,504.4	(1,943.7)
1974	9,085.3	9,372.1	(286.8)
1975	10,948.7	11,902.3	(953.6)
1976	10,729.1	13,278.3	(2,549.2)
1977	8,704.7	12,211.3	(3,506.6)
1978	12,832.9	14,454.7	(1,621.8)
1979	13,089.0	15,923.0	(2,834.0)
1980	19,893.8	21,799.9	(1,906.1)
1981	20,859.7	21,278.3	(418.6)
1982	27,397.2	24,939.6	2,457.6
1983	54,581.7	40,813.9	13,767.8
1984	56,587.9	50,895.0	5,692.9
1985	80,783.1	72,577.3	8,205.8
1986	134,711.0	118,091.9	16,619.1
1987	199,042.0	176,084.9	22,957.1
1988	112,831.8	128,896.2	(16,064.4)
1989	142,965.5	141,748.3	1,217.2
1990	166,753.5	146,743.9	20,009.6
1991	250,734.7	209,536.1	41,198.6
1992	328,330.0	262,121.7	66,208.3
1993	507,808.7	381,334.1	126,474.6
1994	629,628.8	512,992.1	116,636.7

Note: Parentheses indicate net portfolio sales.

Total Purchases, Total Sales, and Net Purchases
of Securities Other Than Common Stocks
by Mutual Funds
1970-1994

(millions of dollars)

Year	Total Purchases	Total Sales	Net Purchases
1970	$3,277.4	$2,687.7	$589.7
1971	3,802.5	3,618.6	183.9
1972	3,524.1	3,270.9	253.2
1973	4,145.9	4,398.7	(252.8)
1974	3,214.4	2,841.4	373.0
1975	4,448.2	3,609.1	839.1
1976	4,619.1	3,602.9	1,016.2
1977	9,463.3	7,209.4	2,253.9
1978	8,112.7	8,615.0	(502.3)
1979	9,323.1	7,779.5	1,543.6
1980	13,093.4	10,280.7	2,812.7
1981	15,302.0	12,430.9	2,871.1
1982	28,284.8	22,981.1	5,303.7
1983	38,427.7	30,652.6	7,775.1
1984	62,684.6	48,034.6	14,650.0
1985	178,795.3	114,397.3	64,398.0
1986	366,347.5	247,075.7	119,271.8
1987	332,033.8	309,555.2	22,478.6
1988	297,882.5	292,553.5	5,329.0
1989	329,253.2	303,982.1	25,271.1
1990	388,946.3	359,804.0	29,142.3
1991	486,037.1	399,372.3	86,664.8
1992	622,302.5	496,850.4	125,452.1
1993	829,248.3	679,704.4	149,543.9
1994	805,501.8	817,279.8	(11,778.0)

Note: Parentheses indicate net portfolio sales.

Portfolio Purchases and Sales by Fund Characteristics
1993-1994

(millions of dollars)

	1993		1994	
	Purchases	Sales	Purchases	Sales
All Securities	**$1,337,057.0**	**$1,061,038.5**	**$1,435,130.6**	**$1,330,271.9**
Method of Sales				
Sales Force	$815,668.4R	$658,265.4R	$854,172.0	$812,617.6
Direct Marketing	432,162.9R	340,310.2R	470,697.0	428,733.1
Variable Annuity	89,020.1R	62,211.9R	110,163.6	88,756.9
Not Offering Shares	205.6	251.0R	98.0	164.3
Investment Objective				
Aggressive Growth	$127,096.5	$110,035.9	$159,571.6	$133,239.4
Growth	137,775.0	117,728.3	169,415.3	152,220.6
Growth & Income	131,303.5	98,041.5	142,999.3	121,422.7
Precious Metals	2,746.7	1,813.8	2,398.2	1,929.5
International	40,842.0	16,438.5	70,902.0	45,351.5
Global Equity	27,470.1	17,430.3	37,616.9	23,716.2
Income-Equity	41,716.8	27,612.3	46,289.8	36,930.9
Flexible Portfolio	27,906.3	17,570.9	36,811.3	30,939.3
Balanced	44,405.8	30,860.5	52,571.1	45,945.9
Income-Mixed	44,587.6	29,473.8	50,064.9	41,983.6
Income-Bond	63,746.5	51,362.1	66,737.2	65,459.3
U.S. Government Income	239,202.3	215,044.6	200,501.0	212,625.8
Ginnie Mae	134,041.0	121,128.8	155,616.7	169,297.6
Global Bond	65,865.5	58,544.7	66,191.5	67,156.3
Corporate Bond	28,285.5	23,046.3	27,544.4	27,006.9
High-yield Bond	46,478.6	35,153.2	35,753.1	34,313.7
National Municipal Bond–Long-term	83,320.6	60,823.1	69,740.3	74,161.8
State Municipal Bond–Long-term	50,266.7	28,929.9	44,406.0	46,570.9
Common Stock Only	**$507,808.7**	**$381,334.1**	**$629,628.8**	**$512,992.1**
Method of Sales				
Sales Force	$224,711.0	$170,844.6	$267,959.6	$218,991.0
Direct Marketing	228,501.4	173,360.8	290,044.4	238,113.0
Variable Annuity	54,393.6	36,887.9	71,527.9	55,724.3
Not Offering Shares	202.7	240.8	96.9	163.8
Investment Objective				
Aggressive Growth	$120,958.6	$103,472.4	$156,027.7	$127,974.6
Growth	133,538.8	113,451.0	158,864.5	142,297.4
Growth & Income	110,626.3	81,534.7	121,152.9	99,845.7
Precious Metals	2,697.0	1,789.8	2,288.1	1,781.2
International	34,658.3	13,174.1	61,965.0	38,754.7
Global Equity	22,518.1	14,593.9	33,614.1	20,692.6
Income-Equity	28,713.0	18,651.3	34,743.2	25,861.2
Flexible Portfolio	17,018.0	10,359.2	19,160.8	17,948.7
Balanced	24,028.8	16,620.1	25,200.8	23,424.1
Income-Mixed	5,974.9	2,438.5	5,271.2	4,428.5
Income-Bond	406.5	321.6	751.4	650.5
U.S. Government Income	17.3	11.6	153.3	219.4
Ginnie Mae	0.0	5.6	0.9	0.0
Global Bond	4,183.5	3,034.2	8,655.6	7,285.7
Corporate Bond	234.4	143.3	95.8	103.6
High-yield Bond	2,215.8	1,713.5	1,681.4	1,701.6
National Municipal Bond–Long-term	6.3	1.7	2.1	22.5
State Municipal Bond–Long-term	13.1	17.6	0.0	0.1

R=Revised

Total Short-term Funds*
1980-1994
(millions of dollars)

Yearend	Total Sales	Total Redemptions	Net Sales	Number of Funds	Total Accounts Outstanding	Total Net Assets
1980	$237,427.7	$207,877.7	$29,550.0	106	4,762,103	$76,361.3
1981	462,422.6	354,972.1	107,450.5	179	10,323,466	186,158.2
1982	611,202.9	580,778.4	30,424.5	318	13,258,143	219,837.5
1983	507,447.0	551,151.3	(43,704.3)	373	12,539,688	179,386.5
1984	634,226.7	586,992.4	47,234.3	421	13,844,697	233,553.8
1985	839,498.8	831,121.2	8,377.6	457	14,934,631R	243,802.4
1986	989,816.0	948,641.3	41,174.7	485	16,313,148	292,151.6
1987	1,060,949.2	1,062,519.7	(1,570.5)	541	17,674,790	316,096.1
1988	1,081,702.0	1,074,373.5	7,328.5	605	18,569,817	337,956.5
1989	1,319,492.6	1,235,643.0	83,849.6	664	21,314,228	428,093.2
1990	1,415,711.8	1,372,713.4	42,998.4	743	22,970,493	498,374.9
1991	1,800,744.7	1,763,094.9	37,649.8	821	23,556,000	542,441.7R
1992	2,386,288.0	2,382,893.3	3,394.7	865	23,647,198	546,194.5R
1993	2,677,539.5	2,673,456.9	4,082.6	920	23,587,257	565,319.1
1994	2,603,330.5	2,598,992.9	4,337.6	963	25,382,690	611,004.5

*Figures are totals for taxable and tax-exempt money market funds. Comparable data for long-term funds can be found on pages 103 and 111.

R = Revised

An Overview: Taxable Money Market Funds
1975-1994

(millions of dollars)

Yearend	Total Sales	Total Redemptions	Net Sales	Number of Funds	Total Accounts Outstanding	Average Maturity (days)	Total Net Assets
1975	$6,748.7	$5,883.9	$864.8	36	208,777	93	$3,695.7
1976	9,360.9	9,609.2	(248.3)	48	180,676	110	3,685.8
1977	10,673.0	10,662.7	10.3	50	177,522	76	3,887.7
1978	30,452.2	24,294.5	6,157.7	61	467,803	42	10,858.0
1979	111,855.1	78,363.4	33,491.7	76	2,307,852	34	45,214.2
1980	232,172.8	204,068.5	28,104.3	96	4,745,572	24	74,447.7
1981	451,889.5	346,701.5	105,188.0	159	10,282,095	34	181,910.4
1982	581,758.9	559,581.1	22,177.8	281	13,101,347	37	206,607.5
1983	462,978.7	508,729.9	(45,751.2)	307	12,276,639	37	162,549.5
1984	571,959.3	531,050.9	40,908.4	329	13,556,180	43	209,731.9
1985	730,073.8	732,343.0	(2,269.2)	346	14,435,386	42	207,535.3
1986	792,349.1	776,303.2	16,045.9	359	15,653,595	40	228,345.8
1987	869,099.1	865,668.4	3,430.7	388	16,832,666	31	254,676.4
1988	903,425.9	899,397.3	4,028.6	431	17,630,528	28	272,293.3
1989	1,134,647.8	1,055,142.4	79,505.4	463	20,173,265	38	358,719.2
1990	1,218,936.0	1,183,065.7	35,870.3	508	21,577,559	41	414,733.3
1991	1,569,852.0	1,536,499.7	33,352.3	554	21,863,352	50	452,559.2
1992	2,099,796.8	2,101,327.8	(1,531.0)	586	21,770,693	51	451,353.4
1993	2,335,653.0	2,336,932.2	(1,279.2)	628	21,586,862	49	461,903.9
1994	2,233,904.8	2,228,905.6	4,999.2	644	23,338,196	34	500,427.8

An Overview: Tax-exempt Money Market Funds
1981-1994

(millions of dollars)

Yearend		Total Sales	Total Redemptions	Net Sales	Number of Funds	Total Accounts Outstanding	Total Net Assets
1981		$10,533.1	$8,270.6	$2,262.5	20	41,371	$4,247.8
1982		29,444.0	22,197.3	7,246.7	37	156,796	13,230.0
1983		44,468.3	42,421.4	2,046.9	66	263,049	16,837.0
1984		62,267.4	55,941.5	6,325.9	95	288,517	23,821.9
1985		109,425.0	98,778.2	10,646.8	111	499,245	36,267.1
1986	National	188,017.3	165,329.1	22,688.2	100	604,055	59,367.5
	State	9,449.7	7,009.1	2,440.6	26	55,498	4,438.2
1987	National	179,215.0	185,031.1	(5,816.1)	111	731,265	54,555.8
	State	12,635.1	11,820.2	814.9	42	110,859	6,863.9
1988	National	158,085.8	158,120.8	(35.0)	120	754,068	54,541.7
	State	20,190.4	16,855.5	3,334.9	54	185,221	11,118.5
1989	National	152,713.4	151,851.4	862.0	129	875,626	52,824.7
	State	32,131.3	28,649.2	3,482.1	72	265,337	16,549.4
1990	National	155,956.9	153,363.8	2,593.1	132	984,301	59,200.5
	State	40,818.9	36,283.9	4,535.0	103	408,633	24,441.1
1991	National	181,137.9	178,927.1	2,210.8	141	1,139,741	62,338.0
	State	49,754.8	47,668.1	2,086.7	126	552,907	27,544.5
1992	National	223,414.2	220,832.0	2,582.2	139	1,120,747	64,863.3
	State	63,077.0	60,733.5	2,343.5	140	755,758	29,977.8
1993	National	264,920.5	261,742.8	3,177.7	146	1,240,257	70,501.3
	State	76,966.0	74,781.9	2,184.1	146	760,138	32,913.9
1994	National	282,293.5	284,070.6	(1,777.1)	157	1,273,384	73,417.8
	State	87,132.2	86,016.7	1,115.5	162	771,110	37,158.9

Taxable Money Market Fund
Monthly Total Net Assets
by Type of Fund

(thousands of dollars)

	Individual	Institutional	Total
1992			
January	$322,210,891	$172,011,602	$494,222,493
February	323,413,887	173,308,527	496,722,414
March	319,035,254	159,239,579	478,274,833
April	313,785,553	169,593,993	483,379,546
May	309,165,774	174,627,496	483,793,270
June	302,550,536	164,227,136	466,777,672
July	302,628,941	190,861,080	493,490,021
August	302,253,484	186,558,876	488,812,360
September	298,421,254	167,182,374	465,603,628
October	303,272,742	179,605,326	482,878,068
November	301,353,282	174,284,429	475,637,711
December	294,307,787	157,045,578	451,353,365
1993			
January	$298,352,439	$183,142,669	$481,495,108
February	301,209,085	180,069,862	481,278,947
March	298,568,342	161,079,923	459,648,265
April	302,046,572	172,077,480	474,124,052
May	300,716,885	171,625,953	472,342,838
June	295,725,143	159,715,741	455,440,884
July	300,761,203	165,455,851	466,217,054
August	297,425,788	164,342,275	461,768,063
September	302,234,978	148,949,143	451,184,121
October	302,405,259	162,072,085	464,477,344
November	312,807,197	159,296,302	472,103,499
December	300,223,605	161,680,266	461,903,871
1994			
January	$303,236,495	$176,678,247	$479,914,742
February	307,635,320	159,507,466	467,142,786
March	314,838,565	152,574,686	467,413,251
April	322,093,585	155,152,506	477,246,091
May	319,282,652	146,723,214	466,005,866
June	317,195,228	148,277,213	465,472,441
July	324,950,414	149,105,393	474,055,807
August	322,882,862	145,831,389	468,714,251
September	327,613,742	148,064,527	475,678,269
October	333,038,139	153,147,231	486,185,370
November	344,716,055	148,824,781	493,540,836
December	344,023,752	156,404,088	500,427,840

Taxable Money Market Fund
Shareholder Accounts by Type of Fund

	Individual	Institutional	Total
1992			
January	22,124,430	204,102	22,328,532
February	22,120,094	211,082	22,331,176
March	22,114,205	227,442	22,341,647
April	22,179,996	230,314	22,410,310
May	22,176,350	232,374	22,408,724
June	22,004,582	235,201	22,239,783
July	22,040,206	234,229	22,274,435
August	22,681,097	229,209	22,910,306
September	21,960,139	227,336	22,187,475
October	22,004,494	215,039	22,219,533
November	21,602,795	219,867	21,822,662
December	21,556,376	214,317	21,770,693
1993			
January	21,719,317	207,343	21,926,660
February	21,747,794	216,649	21,964,443
March	21,780,862	209,795	21,990,657
April	21,878,620	219,898	22,098,518
May	21,942,833	210,429	22,153,262
June	21,679,770	226,216	21,905,986
July	21,772,415	223,217	21,995,632
August	21,623,428	226,012	21,849,440
September	21,701,666	209,015	21,910,681
October	21,568,513	223,812	21,792,325
November	21,731,071	238,732	21,969,803
December	21,338,452	248,410	21,586,862
1994			
January	21,307,967	248,316	21,556,283
February	21,624,012	242,878	21,866,890
March	21,851,325	248,056	22,099,381
April	22,365,137	223,332	22,588,469
May	22,274,155	223,365	22,497,520
June	22,193,718	217,849	22,411,567
July	22,456,048	222,347	22,678,395
August	22,348,011	258,418	22,606,429
September	22,480,195	263,031	22,743,226
October	22,830,425	264,519	23,094,944
November	23,119,607	331,337	23,450,944
December	23,075,051	263,145	23,338,196

Taxable Money Market Fund Asset Composition
Yearend, 1988-1994
(millions of dollars)

	1988	1989	1990	1991	1992	1993	1994
Total Net Assets	$272,293.3	$358,719.2	$414,733.3	$452,559.1	$451,353.4	$461,903.9	$500,427.8
U.S. Treasury Bills	5,110.2	7,352.2	25,471.8	47,645.5	47,284.4	53,188.7	44,348.2
Other Treasury Securities	6,448.4	7,430.3	19,987.1	32,077.5	32,544.6	28,582.7	23,257.9
U.S. Securities	18,376.9	21,040.4	36,892.2	41,387.8	55,254.1	67,985.0	78,863.6
Repurchase Agreements	41,677.1	54,867.7	58,954.8	68,205.7	67,118.3	67,522.4	69,656.2
Commercial Bank CDs[1]	26,601.3	33,593.4	15,932.6	6,281.1	5,313.3	4,339.7	6,712.9
Other Domestic CDs[2]	6,151.1	7,614.0	5,054.7	27,056.8	25,987.2	20,709.4	15,807.8
Eurodollar CDs[3]	29,694.8	26,378.2	27,052.0	21,841.0	20,610.6	10,130.7	16,020.3
Commerical Paper	117,055.8	179,138.9	200,256.0	189,482.0	173,978.1	164,932.4	189,545.5
Bankers' Acceptances	12,035.8	7,468.2	6,433.4	4,611.0	2,664.8	2,320.9	2,431.8
Cash Reserves	661.6	106.6	11,397.6	(211.6)	(2,699.9)	(1,224.7)	(2,575.5)
Other Assets	8,480.3	13,724.3	7,301.1	14,182.3	23,297.9	43,416.7	56,359.1
Average Maturity[4]	28	38	41	50	51	49	34
Number of Funds	431	463	508	554	586	628	644

[1] Commercial bank CDs are those issued by American Banks located in the U.S.
[2] Other domestic CDs include those issued by S&Ls and U.S. branches of foreign banks.
[3] Eurodollar CDs are those issued by foreign branches of domestic banks and some issued by Canadian banks; this category includes some one-day paper.
[4] Maturity of each individual security in the portfolio at the end of month weighted by its value.

Comparable data for long-term funds can be found on page 110.

Sales Due To Exchanges
by Investment Objective
1993-1994

(millions of dollars)

Investment Objective	1993	1994
Aggressive Growth	$28,180.0	$27,663.6
Growth	18,023.7	23,511.4
Growth & Income	16,452.1	15,436.3
Precious Metals	8,201.8	9,004.2
International	12,926.6	22,302.5
Global Equity	5,429.1	11,042.4
Income-Equity	5,543.1	5,638.6
Flexible Portfolio	3,195.8	3,047.1
Balanced	3,540.0	2,991.2
Income-Mixed	4,096.7	3,440.7
Income-Bond	5,798.7	5,724.8
U.S. Government Income	6,868.6	5,208.5
Ginnie Mae	2,937.3	2,618.9
Global Bond	4,309.9	3,339.3
Corporate Bond	2,286.4	1,919.1
High-yield Bond	6,673.9	8,002.2
National Municipal Bond–Long-term	18,332.4	18,952.2
State Municipal Bond–Long-term	6,116.6	9,421.6
Tax-exempt Money Market–National	12,124.6	15,598.5
Tax-exempt Money Market–State	5,642.2	7,459.7
Taxable Money Market	72,342.9	115,387.0

Redemptions Due To Exchanges
by Investment Objective
1993-1994

(millions of dollars)

Investment Objective	1993	1994
Aggressive Growth	$29,524.2	$27,051.2
Growth	20,094.8	22,775.1
Growth & Income	16,522.3	17,855.2
Precious Metals	7,830.6	8,867.2
International	7,081.7	21,415.9
Global Equity	3,418.2	7,371.4
Income-Equity	4,209.7	5,637.1
Flexible Portfolio	1,708.8	3,531.5
Balanced	2,510.9	4,130.0
Income-Mixed	2,341.6	4,477.6
Income-Bond	6,380.4	9,185.1
U.S. Government Income	11,401.0	11,623.9
Ginnie Mae	5,835.9	6,591.0
Global Bond	6,144.4	5,321.6
Corporate Bond	2,452.7	3,325.1
High-yield Bond	5,302.4	10,307.4
National Municipal Bond–Long-term	18,522.9	24,888.3
State Municipal Bond–Long-term	6,301.4	13,941.1
Tax-exempt Money Market–National	11,482.5	13,385.0
Tax-exempt Money Market–State	5,053.6	6,019.7
Taxable Money Market	80,178.9	7,870.6

Net Sales Due To Exchanges
by Investment Objective
1993-1994

(millions of dollars)

Investment Objective	1993	1994
Aggressive Growth	$(1,344.2)	$612.4
Growth	(2,071.1)	736.3
Growth & Income	(70.2)	(2,418.9)
Precious Metals	371.2	137.0
International	5,844.9	886.6
Global Equity	2,010.9	3,671.0
Income-Equity	1,333.4	1.5
Flexible Portfolio	1,487.0	(484.4)
Balanced	1,029.1	(1,138.8)
Income-Mixed	1,755.1	(1,036.9)
Income-Bond	(581.7)	(3,460.3)
U.S. Government Income	(4,532.4)	(6,415.4)
Ginnie Mae	(2,898.6)	(3,972.1)
Global Bond	(1,834.5)	(1,982.3)
Corporate Bond	(166.3)	(1,406.0)
High-yield Bond	1,371.5	(2,305.2)
National Municipal Bond–Long-term	(190.5)	(5,936.1)
State Municipal Bond–Long-term	(184.8)	(4,519.5)
Tax-exempt Money Market–National	642.1	2,213.5
Tax-exempt Money Market–State	588.6	1,440.0
Taxable Money Market	(7,836.0)	17,516.4

IRA Assets and Accounts
by Investment Objective
Yearend 1994

Investment Objective	Assets		Accounts	
	Millions of Dollars	Percent	Number (thousands)	Percent
Aggressive Growth	$23,160.9	8.1%	3,158.0	10.2%
Growth	42,830.1	15.0	4,906.9	15.8
Growth & Income	41,843.9	14.7	4,016.0	12.9
Precious Metals	1,346.3	0.5	247.3	0.8
International	12,473.5	4.4	1,712.8	5.5
Global Equity	13,248.3	4.6	1,632.5	5.2
Income-Equity	18,749.3	6.6	1,944.2	6.3
Flexible Portfolio	7,996.5	2.8	816.7	2.6
Balanced	13,335.9	4.7	1,291.2	4.2
Income-Mixed	13,225.1	4.6	974.1	3.1
Income-Bond	6,634.0	2.3	494.2	1.6
U.S. Government Income	14,180.0	5.0	1,105.4	3.6
Ginnie Mae	8,170.0	2.9	664.3	2.1
Global Bond	1,885.3	0.6	189.7	0.6
Corporate Bond	5,639.5	2.0	400.8	1.3
High-yield Bond	9,123.8	3.2	793.2	2.5
Taxable Money Market	51,384.5	18.0	6,752.2	21.7
Total	**$285,226.9**	**100.0%**	**31,099.5**	**100.0%**

Self-employed Retirement Plan Assets and Accounts by Investment Objective
Yearend 1994

Investment Objective	Assets		Accounts	
	Millions of Dollars	Percent	Number (thousands)	Percent
Aggressive Growth	$907.5	2.6%	61.4	4.5%
Growth	4,395.4	12.6	163.8	11.9
Growth & Income	8,340.4	24.0	214.2	15.6
Precious Metals	68.1	0.2	7.1	0.5
International	2,669.0	7.7	83.1	6.1
Global Equity	2,595.5	7.5	112.6	8.2
Income-Equity	839.1	2.4	40.9	3.0
Flexible Portfolio	332.1	1.0	16.4	1.2
Balanced	1,132.1	3.3	29.1	2.1
Income-Mixed	1,722.7	4.9	57.7	4.2
Income-Bond	1,444.2	4.1	42.0	3.1
U.S. Government Income	728.6	2.1	31.2	2.3
Ginnie Mae	297.9	0.9	16.4	1.2
Global Bond	213.8	0.6	11.7	0.8
Corporate Bond	532.9	1.5	18.9	1.4
High-yield Bond	411.6	1.2	21.7	1.6
Taxable Money Market	8,147.4	23.4	443.7	32.3
Total	**$34,778.3**	**100.0%**	**1,371.9**	**100.0%**

Number of Accounts of Fiduciary, Business, and Institutional Investors in Equity and Bond & Income Funds

	1989	1990	1991	1992	1993	1994
Fiduciaries (Banks & Individuals Serving as Trustees, Guardians, & Administrators)	2,696,987	3,538,438	3,706,706	4,991,706	6,498,972	8,084,072
Business Corporations	131,039	131,723	145,135	193,906	234,412	296,970
Retirement Plans	1,767,939	1,999,287	2,332,763	3,108,029	4,373,959R	5,161,769
Insurance Companies & Other Financial Institutions	74,799	85,577	29,915	43,182	69,929	122,573
Unions	1,736	2,582	9,197	3,942	2,489	6,164
Total Business Organizations	1,975,513	2,219,169	2,517,010	3,349,059	4,680,789R	5,587,476
Churches & Religious Organizations	17,257	18,470	25,289	29,651	46,387	44,411
Fraternal, Welfare & Other Public Associations	10,830	10,753	16,948	15,189	21,790	24,592
Hospitals, Sanitariums, Orphanages, etc.	3,168	5,059	3,957	4,837	10,436	4,661
Schools & Colleges	6,407	6,328	5,743	7,486	13,946	10,844
Foundations	2,986	5,335	5,220	5,134	15,340	10,098
Total Institutions & Foundations	40,648	45,945	57,157	62,297	107,899	94,606
Other Institutional Investors Not Classified (a)	249,814	201,738	326,091	486,858	699,315	1,217,492
Total	4,962,962	6,005,290	6,606,964	8,889,920	11,986,975R	14,983,646

(a) Includes institutional accounts which do not fall under other classifications and those for which no determination of classification can be made.

Note: Reporters of institutional data represented 83.8% of total shareholder accounts in 1989, 82.3% in 1990, 82.4% in 1991, 83.5% in 1992, 84.0% in 1993 and 78.8% in 1994.

R—Revised

Assets of Fiduciary, Business, and Institutional Investors in Equity and Bond & Income Funds

(millions of dollars)

	1989	1990	1991	1992	1993	1994
Fiduciaries (Banks & Individuals Serving as Trustees, Guardians, & Administrtors)	$57,924.5	$62,715.4	$93,635.2	$127,530.6	$183,471.4	$200,895.2
Business Corporations	11,709.5	9,723.2	14,828.0	21,148.1	29,776.2	31,061.0
Retirement Plans	41,573.3	45,353.6	64,420.7	130,148.1	200,350.3R	213,014.2
Insurance Companies & Other Financial Institutions	19,137.6	30,689.8	45,878.4	70,710.0	112,258.5	115,816.1
Unions	509.7	346.8	391.1	455.6	763.1	900.8
Total Business Organizations	$72,930.1	$86,113.4	$125,518.2	$222,461.8	$343,148.2R	$360,792.0
Churches & Religious Organizations	1,100.8	952.3	1,694.7	2,080.0	2,820.9	4,0872
Fraternal, Welfare & Other Public Associations	900.3	1,160.3	1,027.1	1,275.5	2,548.3	2,654.0
Hospitals, Sanitariums, Orphanages, etc.	409.7	415.2	587.6	803.6	1,268.8	1,109.8
Schools & Colleges	733.1	853.3	717.4	1,142.5	1,516.0	2,009.4
Foundations	519.9	548.7	1,778.2	1,386.4	2,478.8	2,637.9
Total Institutions & Foundations	$3,663.8	$3,929.8	$5,805.0	$6,688.0	$10,632.8	$12,498.3
Other Institutional Investors Not Classified (a)	$9,443.2	$9,535.3	$14,532.5	$23,942.7	$26,752.7	$32,939.5
Total	$143,961.6	$162,293.9	$239,490.9	$380,623.1	$564,005.1R	$607,124.9

(a) Includes institutional total net assets which do not fall under other classifications and those for which no determination of classification can be made.

Note: Reporters of institutional data represented 83.3% of total shareholder total net assets in 1989, 83.0% in 1990, 80.9% in 1991, 85.8% in 1992, 85.0% in 1993 and 79.7% in 1994.

R=Revised

Number of Accounts of Fiduciary, Business, and Institutional Investors in Taxable Money Market Funds

	1989	1990	1991	1992	1993	1994
Fiduciaries (Banks & Individuals Serving as Trustees, Guardians, & Administrators)	**840,248**	**909,720**	**950,781**	**1,021,682**	**984,959**	**1,641,291**
Business Corporations	237,278	272,321	213,283	280,480	219,491	272,250
Retirement Plans	693,782	781,699	828,714	635,911	704,337	847,991
Insurance Companies & Other Financial Institutions	34,234	49,268	26,961	31,002	50,188	97,760
Unions	1,921	1,784	2,284	1,781	1,568	2,761
Total Business Organizations	**967,215**	**1,105,072**	**1,071,242**	**949,174**	**975,584**	**1,220,762**
Churches & Religious Organizations	15,314	18,693	22,201	24,100	23,397	22,310
Fraternal, Welfare & Other Public Associations	10,204	11,120	10,169	11,121	9,250	23,174
Hospitals, Sanitariums, Orphanages, etc.	3,216	5,014	4,247	4,468	5,118	5,003
Schools & Colleges	3,756	4,173	4,412	6,432	4,455	12,172
Foundations	1,922	4,112	7,109	6,655	5,402	4,223
Total Institutions & Foundations	**34,412**	**43,112**	**48,138**	**52,776**	**47,622**	**66,882**
Other Institutional Investors Not Classified (a)	**101,065**	**55,879**	**69,180**	**83,322**	**138,849**	**247,023**
Total	**1,942,940**	**2,113,783**	**2,139,341**	**2,106,954**	**2,147,014**	**3,175,958**

(a) Includes institutional accounts which do not fall under other classifications and those for which no determination of classification can be made.

Note: Reporters of institutional data represented 63.8% of total shareholder accounts in 1989, 62.0% in 1990, 64.4% in 1991, 66.2% in 1992, 58.2% in 1993 and 61.5% in 1994.

Number of Accounts of Fiduciary, Business, and Institutional Investors in Taxable Money Market Funds by Type of Fund

	Individual		Institutional	
	1993	1994	1993	1994
Fiduciaries (Banks & Individuals Serving as Trustees, Guardians, & Administrators)	**928,742**	**1,605,868**	**56,217**	**35,423**
Business Corporations	205,986	256,978	13,505	15,272
Retirement Plans	666,491	796,523	37,846	51,468
Insurance Companies & Other Financial Institutions	47,270	94,734	2,918	3,026
Unions	1,428	2,440	140	321
Total Business Organizations	**921,175**	**1,150,675**	**54,409**	**70,087**
Churches & Religious Organizations	22,650	20,725	747	1,585
Fraternal, Welfare & Other Public Associations	9,051	22,729	199	445
Hospitals, Sanitariums, Orphanages etc.	3,551	4,527	1,567	476
Schools & College	3,980	11,265	475	907
Foundations	5,249	3,998	153	225
Total Institutions & Foundations	**44,481**	**63,244**	**3,141**	**3,638**
Other Institutional Investors Not Classified (a)	**133,043**	**227,816**	**5,806**	**19,207**
Total	**2,027,441**	**3,047,603**	**119,573**	**128,355**

(a) Includes institutional accounts which do not fall under other classifications and those for which no determination of classification can be made.

Number of Accounts of Fiduciary, Business, and Institutional Investors in Tax-exempt Money Market Funds

	1989	1990	1991	1992	1993	1994
Fiduciaries (Banks & Individuals Serving as Trustees, Guardians, & Administrators)	**102,939**	**132,326**	**129,806**	**124,996**	**158,814**	**242,762**
Business Corporations	10,395	13,436	16,831	16,573	18,924	19,442
Retirement Plans	13,312	11,977	15,035	2,286	3,577	5,487
Insurance Companies & Other Financial Institutions	1,868	2,074	972	1,262	3,363	3,996
Unions	56	66	196	68	6	31
Total Business Organizations	**25,631**	**27,553**	**33,034**	**20,189**	**25,870**	**28,956**
Churches & Religious Organizations	35	32	73	64	208	190
Fraternal, Welfare & Other Public Associations	62	109	132	117	128	209
Hospitals, Sanitariums, Orphanages, etc.	34	45	34	47	67	74
Schools & Colleges	52	74	65	70	92	113
Foundations	38	26	105	59	222	280
Total Institutions & Foundations	**221**	**286**	**409**	**357**	**717**	**866**
Other Institutional Investors Not Classified (a)	**11,577**	**5,617**	**6,290**	**5,078**	**6,514**	**10,143**
Total	**140,368**	**165,782**	**169,539**	**150,620**	**191,915**	**282,727**

(a) Includes institutional accounts which do not fall under other classifications and those for which no determination of classification can be made.

Note: Tax-exempt Money Market fund reporters represented 73.4% of total shareholder accounts in 1989, 78.3% in 1990, 62.8% in 1991, 68.6% in 1992, 59.7% in 1993 and 53.3% in 1994

Assets of Fiduciary, Business, and Institutional Investors in Taxable Money Market Funds

(millions of dollars)

	1989	1990	1991	1992	1993	1994
Fiduciaries (Banks & Individuals Serving as Trustees, Guardians, & Administrators)	**$100,830.0**	**$96,488.2**	**$101,878.9**	**$104,973.1**	**$118,920.6**	**$125,535.5**
Business Corporations	13,720.6	22,839.5	27,559.1	41,498.1	37,954.0	45,789.9
Retirement Plans	16,679.0	21,062.9	21,312.1	22,852.9	30,132.8	35,189.6
Insurance Companies & Other Financial Institutions	5,787.0	17,190.9	23,639.8	29,115.6	34,939.1	22,646.0
Unions	208.4	421.9	141.7	340.7	250.1	176.2
Total Business Organizations	**$36,395.0**	**$61,515.2**	**$72,652.7**	**$93,807.3**	**$103,276.0**	**$103,801.6**
Churches & Religious Organizations	962.5	743.4	865.6	789.8	760.6	1,626.5
Fraternal, Welfare & Other Public Associations	457.7	966.1	559.1	1,030.2	879.3	1,304.0
Hospitals, Sanitariums, Orphanages, etc.	320.4	628.9	720.3	1,207.5	1,574.7	812.4
Schools & Colleges	306.4	397.8	746.1	493.8	530.5	864.8
Foundations	288.1	584.2	615.2	523.8	448.1	567.9
Total Institutions & Foundations	**$2,335.1**	**$3,320.4**	**$3,506.3**	**$4,045.1**	**$4,193.2**	**$5,175.7**
Other Institutional Investors Not Classified (a)	**$5,876.7**	**$10,728.4**	**$12,264.2**	**$14,487.8**	**$17,682.6**	**$18,858.4**
Total	**$145,436.8**	**$172,052.2**	**$190,302.1**	**$217,313.3**	**$244,072.4**	**$253,371.3**

(a) Includes institutional assets which do not fall under other classifications and those for which no determination of classification can be made.

Note: Reporters of institutional data represented 61.7% of total net assets in 1989, 64.5% in 1990, 70.5% in 1991, 62.4% in 1992, 60.2% in 1993 and 58.2% in 1994.

Assets of Fiduciary, Business, and Institutional Investors in Taxable Money Market Funds by Type of Fund

(millions of dollars)

	Individual		Institutional	
	1993	1994	1993	1994
Fiduciaries (Banks & Individuals Serving as Trustees, Guardians & Administrators)	$42,980.0	$53,000.4	$75,940.6	$72,535.1
Business Corporations	17,007.4	20,088.6	20,946.6	25,701.3
Retirement Plans	18,531.3	17,955.7	11,601.5	17,233.9
Insurance Companies & Other Financial Institutions	6,438.5	4,476.0	28,500.5	18,170.0
Unions	145.5	142.3	104.6	33.9
Total Business Organizations	$42,122.8	$42,662.7	$61,153.2	61,139.0
Churches & Religious Organizations	695.0	1,000.3	65.7	626.2
Fraternal, Welfare & Other Public Associations	248.4	1,091.2	630.9	212.8
Hospitals, Sanitariums, Orphanages etc.	515.9	395.5	1,058.6	416.9
Schools & Colleges	188.4	505.8	342.2	359.0
Foundations	338.3	324.9	109.8	243.0
Total Institutions & Foundations	$1,986.0	$3,317.7	$2,207.2	$1,858.0
Other Institutional Investors Not Classified (a)	$7,143.4	$9,918.3	$10,539.2	$8,940.1
Total	$94,232.2	$108,899.1	$149,840.2	$144,472.2

(a) Includes institutional accounts which do not fall under other classifications and those for which no determination of classification can be made.

Assets of Fiduciary, Business, and Institutional Investors in Tax-exempt Money Market Funds

(millions of dollars)

	1989	1990	1991	1992	1993	1994
Fiduciaries (Banks & Individuals Serving as Trustees, Guardians, & Administrators)	$18,421.9	$21,664.3	$22,713.4	$23,729.6	$22,830.2	$25,236.6
Business Corporations	2,432.8	3,481.3	4,755.5	5,848.2	6,858.2	6,418.5
Retirement Plans	773.5	460.3	672.1	672	309.3	708.9
Insurance Companies & Other Financial Institutions	424.8	874.3	1,344.8	1,168.4	1,777.8	1,482.8
Unions	3.3	17.8	12.8	3.0	1.3	0.6
Total Business Organizations	$3,634.4	$4,833.7	$6,785.2	$7,086.8	$8,946.6	$8,610.9
Churches & Religious Organizations	7.4	13.5	3.8	4.2	7.2	1.4
Fraternal, Welfare & Other Public Associations	2.7	20.4	12.6	11.8	7.2	16.7
Hospitals, Sanitariums, Orphanages, etc.	9.2	17.1	4.1	6.4	11.4	38.8
Schools & Colleges	10.9	20.0	11.6	4.6	6.3	8.4
Foundations	3.8	13.8	6.6	4.0	6.9	9.7
Total Institutions & Foundations	$34.0	$84.8	$38.7	$31.0	$39.0	$74.9
Other Institutional Investors Not Classified (a)	$920.1	$1,053.6	$2,625.5	$1,907.9	$1,123.5	$3,161.1
Total	$23,010.4	$27,636.4	$32,162.8	$32,755.3	$32,939.3	$37,083.5

(a) Includes institutional total net assets which do not fall under other classifications and those for which no determination of classification can be made.

Note: Tax-exempt Money Market fund reporters represented 63.3% of total net assets in 1989, 69.0% in 1990, 63.2% in 1991, 68.9% in 1992, 60.3% in 1993 and 54.4% in 1994.

Assets of Major Institutions and Financial Intermediaries

(millions of dollars)

	1987	1988	1989	1990	1991	1992	1993	1994
Depository Institutions								
Commercial Banks	$2,774,400R	$2,952,400R	$3,232,000R	$3,338,600R	$3,443,400R	$3,657,000R	$3,896,100R	$4,161,700
Credit Unions[a]	178,200	192,300	201,700	217,000	239,500	263,900	280,900R	294,600
Savings Institutions[b]	1,505,100R	1,640,500R	1,512,600R	1,357,700R	1,172,000R	1,078,800R	1,029,500R	1,013,100
Life Insurance	**$1,005,300**	**$1,132,900**	**$1,260,200**	**$1,367,400**	**$1,505,300**	**$1,614,300**	**$1,784,900R**	**$1,887,900**
Investment Institutions								
Bank Administered Trusts[c]	$1,085,078	$1,156,782	$1,328,481	$1,368,666	$1,585,406	$1,791,526	$2,050,122	N/A
Closed-end Investment Companies	21,478	43,259	53,626	52,657R	74,765R	94,263R	110,872R	116,033[d]
Mutual Funds[e]	769,939	810,250	981,955	1,066,892	1,395,498	1,646,259	2,075,366	2,161,495

[a]Includes only federal or federally insured state credit unions serving natural persons
[b]Includes mutual savings banks, federal savings banks, and savings & loan associations
[c]Reflects only discretionary trusts and agencies
[d]Preliminary number
[e]Includes short-term funds

N/A = Not available

R = Revised

Index

D

E

F

G

H

L

M

N

O

P

R

S

T

More Information on Mutual Funds

*With the exception of the **Fact Book**, the **Directory of Mutual Funds**, and the brochure, **Matching Mutual Funds to Your Needs and Goals**, single copies of brochures ordered by the general public are free; multiple copies (maximum of 30) ordered by schools, clubs, and public libraries are also available at no charge, provided that orders are received on the organization's letterhead. To request single copies or paid orders of brochures, the **Directory**, or the **Fact Book**, please use the order form on page 157. For information on volume quantities, please call the Institute at 202/326-5872. For information on imprinting brochures, call 202/326-5887.*

What Is a Mutual Fund? 8 FUNDamentals
This concise, illustrated leaflet reveals eight key features of a mutual fund investment. Included is an illustration showing how to read newspaper mutual fund tables and a chart illustrating the risk/return tradeoff. *25 cents each*

Discipline. It Can't Really Be Good for You, Can It?
Dollar-cost averaging, the strategy of buying more when the price of mutual fund shares is low and buying less when the price is high, is explained in this colorful leaflet. Examples show how dollar-cost averaging works when the market fluctuates, declines, and rises. *20 cents each*

Eight Basics of Bond Fund Investing
This brochure explains why bond mutual fund investments have become such favorites in recent years. Eight considerations for any bond fund investor—new or experienced—are discussed. Demystifies yield, total return, and investment risks, including inflation risk. Includes charts that compare eight different types of bond funds and show the risk/return tradeoff. *30 cents each*

Investing: Start Now! (It's later than you think.)
This colorful leaflet illustrates the time value of money. Two eye-opening examples show how less money invested now can become more valuable than more money invested later. *20 cents each*

An Investor's Guide to Reading the Mutual Fund Prospectus

Finally, a brochure that deciphers the "legalese" of mutual fund prospectuses. This colorfully illustrated brochure takes you on a guided tour of the 18 most important items you're likely to encounter in prospectuses. Using sample language from actual prospectuses, the brochure describes how each item affects you, what to look for, and why. *40 cents each*

Matching Mutual Funds to Your Needs and Goals

This "slide guide" allows you to match your investment objectives with various types of mutual funds. Included are typical investor profiles. *$1.00 each*

Money Market Mutual Funds—A Part of Every Financial Plan

In easy-to-understand language, this brochure explores money market funds—an investment that changed the way Americans handle their money. Explains why millions of Americans looking for safety, liquidity, and yield turn to money market funds. *25 cents each*

Mutual Funds: Creating Solutions for Small Company Retirement Plans

This colorful, 16-page brochure explains how mutual funds can help owners of small and mid-size businesses offer retirement plans to their employees. Among the topics explored are the benefits of retirement plans, the fiduciary responsibilities of a retirement plan sponsor, what Section 404(c) of ERISA means for retirement plan sponsors, and how mutual funds can help small and mid-size business owners comply with Section 404(c). *25 cents each*

Planning for College? The Mutual Fund Advantage Becomes a Parent

The value of a college education is well-known. This brochure offers practical insights to those preparing to meet the rising costs of a college education and outlines the major advantages of mutual funds in meeting those costs. Information on the latest tax rules for minors is included. *25 cents each*

Retirement Plan Distributions: Easing the Tax Bite

This leaflet explains why employees leaving their jobs should arrange to transfer their retirement plan distributions directly into another qualified plan or IRA. Tax and penalty consequences of acting otherwise are explored through examples. Concludes with a brief summary of the advantages of investing in mutual funds for retirement. *20 cents each*

Time to Celebrate Life: Investing for Retirement with Mutual Funds

This retirement primer explains why Americans need to plan for retirement. Among the types of retirement plans described are 401(k) plans, 403(b) plans, Keoghs, Individual Retirement Accounts (IRAs), and Simplified Employee Pension Plans (SEPs). The benefits that mutual funds offer individuals and employers are also discussed. *45 cents each*

A Close Look at Closed-end Funds

This brochure examines why closed-end funds have become an increasingly popular investment choice. Describes common types of closed-end funds, how they differ from open-end (mutual) funds, and how to select and purchase shares. *25 cents each*

On Track with Unit Investment Trusts

Unit investment trusts, which are fixed portfolios of preselected bonds or stocks, offer investors an attractive alternative to direct purchases of securities. This brochure examines how UITs work, the various types available, and describes the benefits of UIT investments. *25 cents each*

Tax Dos and Don'ts for Mutual Fund Investors

This brochure offers 13 tax tips for mutual fund investors. Contains easy-to-understand discussions of taxable distributions paid to fund shareholders, Form 1099-DIV, the tax effect of reinvesting dividends and exchanging shares, the advantages of tax-exempt funds, plus examples of adjustments to cost basis, and more. *35 cents each*

Directory of Mutual Funds

In addition to fund names, addresses, and telephone numbers (many toll-free), the directory lists each fund's assets, initial and subsequent investment requirements, the year the fund began, where to buy shares, and other pertinent details. The funds are categorized by their investment objectives. An introductory text serves as a "short course" in mutual fund investing. *358 pages, $8.50 each*

Mutual Fund Fact Book

Annually updated facts and figures on the U.S. mutual fund industry, including trends in sales, assets, and performance. Outlines history and growth of the fund industry, its policies, operations, regulation, services, and shareholders. *158 pages, $25.00 each*

Speaker Referral Service

The Institute can help you find a leading mutual fund executive to address your group, class, or meeting. In a generic, educational presentation, your group can learn the basics of mutual fund investing, the types and benefits of funds, the factors to consider when selecting a fund, and more. Speakers are available in most areas of the country. Call Tracy Weiland at 202/326-5871 for more information. *No charge*

Order Form for Brochures and Publications

The Institute also offers a variety of films, videos, and slides on mutual funds. Call 202/326-5872 or check the box below for a catalog. All prices include shipping and handling, although postage will be billed for overseas shipments exceeding 4 lbs. Volume quantities will be shipped via UPS. Payment must accompany all orders, and **please make checks payable to Investment Company Institute.** *All checks must be drawn on United States banks; no foreign checks will be accepted. The Investment Company Institute also accepts Visa and Mastercard orders, although we request that you send a check for orders less than $10. Please allow three weeks for delivery.*

	Unit Cost	Quantity	Total
What Is a Mutual Fund? 8 FUNDamentals	$ .25		
Discipline. It Can't Really Be Good for You, Can It?	.20		
Eight Basics of Bond Fund Investing	.30		
Investing: Start Now! (It's later than you think.)	.20		
An Investor's Guide to Reading the Mutual Fund Prospectus	.40		
Matching Mutual Funds to Your Needs and Goals	1.00		
Money Market Mutual Funds–A Part of Every Financial Plan	.25		
Mutual Funds: Creating Solutions for Small Company Retirement Plans	.25		
Planning for College? The Mutual Fund Advantage Becomes a Parent	.25		
Retirement Plan Distributions: Easing the Tax Bite	.20		
Time to Celebrate Life: Investing for Retirement with Mutual Funds	.45		
A Close Look at Closed-end Funds	.25		
On Track with Unit Investment Trusts	.25		
Tax Dos & Don'ts for Mutual Fund Investors	.35		
Directory of Mutual Funds	8.50		
Mutual Fund Fact Book	25.00		
TOTAL COST			

☐ *Yes! I would like more information about mutual funds. Please send me the publications catalog.*
Please print clearly and return the order form and a check to: Michelle Worthy, Investment Company Institute, 1401 H Street, NW, Suite 1200, Washington, DC 20005.

Name

Company

Street Address *(Please do not use a P.O. Box number or rural route address. UPS will not deliver to these addresses.)*

City, State, Zip

Telephone *(Required for credit card orders; include area code)*

Credit card name (Visa or Mastercard), Card number, Expiration date

Signature